THE POWER & LIFE OF THE WORD

LAWSON PERDUE

Charis
CHRISTIAN CENTER

TABLE OF CONTENTS

TABLE OF CONTENTS i

INTRODUCTION.. 1

PART ONE: BELIEVE IT TO RECEIVE IT 7
   CHAPTER ONE 9
    OUR ATTITUDE TOWARD THE WORD
   CHAPTER TWO 15
    RECEIVING THE WORD WITH MEEKNESS
   CHAPTER THREE 23
    USING WHAT WE HAVE
   CHAPTER FOUR 33
    DOUBT: THE ENEMY OF OUR FAITH

PART TWO: RENEWING OUR MINDS 43
   CHAPTER FIVE 45
    SEEING THINGS FROM GOD'S PERSPECTIVE
   CHAPTER SIX 57
    THE WORD IS SEED
   CHAPTER SEVEN 65
    THE CONCEPTION PERIOD
   CHAPTER EIGHT 73
    A PICTURE LIKE THE WORD

PART THREE: THE PURPOSE OF THE WORD 83
   CHAPTER NINE 85
    THE WORD IS FOOD
   CHAPTER TEN 93
    THE WORD IS OUR DEFENSE
   CHAPTER ELEVEN 103
    THE WORD IS OUR OFFENSE

Introduction

The Word of God is full of promises: promises for our health, our safety, our prosperity, our peace—promises for every area of our lives. But just knowing that those promises exist is not enough. Without an accurate picture of who God is, and an understanding of how to receive from Him, we can hinder the power and life of the Word from producing a harvest in our lives.

Psalm 68 tells us that God daily loads us with benefits![1] But how do we realize those in our lives? How do we see the promises of God made manifest? If God's Word is true,[2] and He does not change,[3] then we should expect His Word to come to pass. If we are not seeing the truth of the Word play out in our daily lives, then perhaps we have not recognized *our* part to play in receiving the blessings God has for us.

To truly experience the power and life of the Word, we must begin to recognize the faithfulness and authority of it as the very Words of God.

It is more than just a history book! God's Word is a part of Himself. It is spirit, as He is, and It continues into eternity, as He does.

> *The Spirit alone gives eternal life. Human effort accomplishes nothing. And the very words I have spoken to you are spirit and life.*
>
> John 6:63 (NLT)

> *Long ago I learned from your written instructions that you made them to last forever.*
>
> Psalm 119:152 (God's Word)

> *The grass withers, the flower fades: but the word of our God shall stand forever.*
>
> Isaiah 40:8

> *Heaven and earth will pass away, but my words will never pass away.*
>
> Mark 13:31

Not only is God's Word eternal and steadfast, but it also reveals His character and covenant to us. It shows us His good plan and purpose for our lives.

> *This is what the LORD says--your Redeemer, the Holy One of Israel: "I am the LORD your God, who teaches you what is best for you, who directs you in the way you should go.*
>
> Isaiah 48:17 (NIV)

> *My covenant will I not break, nor alter the thing that is gone out of my lips.*
>
> Psalm 89:34

> *For I know the plans I have for you," declares the LORD, "plans to prosper you and not to harm you, plans to give you hope and a future."*
>
> Jeremiah 29:11 (NIV)

Knowing who God is and what He thinks of us—knowing His Word—produces faith. It is by faith that we receive everything His Grace has provided!

*So then faith comes by hearing, and hearing by
the word of God.*

Romans 10:17

For by grace ye are saved through faith.

Ephesians 2:8

*Therefore, the promise comes by faith, so that it
may be by grace and may be guaranteed to all
Abraham's offspring.*

Romans 4:16 (NIV)

*Therefore, being justified by faith, we have peace
with God through our Lord Jesus Christ, by whom
also we have access by faith into this grace
wherein we stand, and we rejoice in the hope of
the glory of God.*

Romans 5:1-2

When we allow the Word of God to teach us, and learn
to respond to that Word with faith, we will "see the goodness
of God in the land of the living."[4]

There is a great example of this in the life of Jeremiah.
God had a special plan for Jeremiah's life, but He had to
teach Jeremiah how to bring that plan to fruition.

*Then the word of the LORD came unto me,
saying, 'Before I formed you in the womb I knew
you; and before you came forth out of the womb
I sanctified you, and I ordained you a prophet
unto the nations.' Then said I, 'Ah, Lord GOD!
behold, I cannot speak: for I am a child.' But the
LORD said unto me, 'Say not, I am a child: for you
shall go to all that I shall send you, and
whatsoever I command you, you shall speak. Be
not afraid of their faces: for I am with you to
deliver you, says the LORD.' Then the LORD put*

> *forth his hand, and touched my mouth. And the LORD said unto me, 'Behold, I have put my words in your mouth. See, I have this day set you over the nations and over the kingdoms, to root out, and to pull down, and to destroy, and to throw down, to build, and to plant.' Moreover the word of the LORD came unto me, saying, 'Jeremiah, what see you?' And I said,' I see a rod of an almond tree.' Then said the LORD unto me, 'You have well seen: for I will hasten my word to perform it'*

> Jeremiah 1:4-12

Notice, the *Word of the Lord* came to Jeremiah and said, "Before I formed you in the belly, I knew you…I chose you to be a prophet to the nations." God had a purpose for Jeremiah's life, and He revealed it to him through His Word. But when we continue reading, we notice Jeremiah's idea of himself did not match up with God's.

Jeremiah said, "Lord, I am only a child." God rebuked Jeremiah for disagreeing with His Word. He challenged him to believe the Word that was spoken about him. When Jeremiah began to believe, or put faith in what God said, he started fulfilling God's purpose for his life.

God has a purpose and plan for your life too! It is a good plan, and He wants to reveal it to you through His Word. But you must be willing to learn, to be corrected, and to change your natural thoughts and ideas, just like Jeremiah did.

Even though Jeremiah did not initially accept God's Word, God was able to correct him and redirect his thoughts because he respected the Word of God. Jeremiah received correction, changed his own ideas of himself, and began to see himself the way God saw him.

We have to understand, like Jeremiah, that God's Word is truth, and that Truth is not relative. It does not change because of time or circumstances;[5] it is constant. By putting ourselves in submission to the Word we are made steadfast: the winds of doctrine, society, and temptation do not move us.[6] Satan cannot shake our confidence.[7] We are planted and in position to receive the benefits of the covenant promised in God's Word!

---

[1] Psalm 68:19 New King James Version
[2] Numbers 23:19; Psalm 119:160
[3] Hebrews 13:8; James 1:17
[4] Psalm 27:13
[5] Psalm 199:160; Psalm 18:30
[6] Ephesians 4:14
[7] 1 John 3:21

PART ONE

BELIEVE IT TO RECEIVE IT

Jesus said unto him, "If you can believe, all things are possible to him that believeth."

Mark 9:23

CHAPTER ONE

OUR ATTITUDE TOWARD THE WORD

The Word of God is full of life and power. It holds the same power as does God Himself: It is part of Him. Scripture tells us that God and His Word are one.[1] It says that God has exalted His Word above everything,[2] and that it is by the Word of His power all things were created and are held together.[3] But just knowing the Word of God is full of power does not produce life within us. We must go further; we must believe. Jesus said,

> *"If you can believe, all things are possible to him that believes."*
>
> Mark 9:23

What does it mean to believe? Part of believing is having a correct attitude toward the Word. David had a great attitude toward the Word. In Psalm 19, he says that the "law (or Word) of the Lord is perfect, reviving the soul."[4] He is saying the Word is complete; It does not lack in any area, but it can refresh, or quicken, the soul. It is the Word of God that produces life.

We need to have that same attitude toward the Word. We need to say from our hearts, "Whatever You say God. Your Word is true!" If that's our attitude, it will cause us to live lives directed by the Word.

The Word of God gives us clear instructions about how to live. It shows us God's way of justice and mercy,[5] and the results of living for ourselves.[6] It tells us the best ways to conduct ourselves and deal peacefully and right with men. We must have an attitude that says, "If I see it in the Word, then that's what I'm going to believe, that's how I'm going to operate." Too often, we become willing to compromise the instructions of the Word when circumstances seem difficult or when we're feeling challenged by society. We can't do that. We must determine that we will live our lives by the directives of the Word.

Let's take a look at Second Peter. At the beginning of this book, Peter is describing his relationship with Jesus, the Word made flesh,[7] and he says,

> *For we have not followed cunningly devised fables when we made known to you the power and the coming of our Lord Jesus Christ, but we were eyewitnesses of His majesty. For He received from God the Father glory and honor, when there came a voice from His excellent glory, 'this is My beloved Son in whom I am well pleased.' And this voice which came from heaven we heard, when we were with him in the holy mount.*
>
> 2 Peter 1:16-18 (NKJV)

Peter says, "We haven't followed storybook characters; we're not talking about made up legends. We were there! We're telling you about Jesus the Christ, God's own Son!

We're talking about having a personal relationship with God in the flesh!"

Peter is referring to the time recorded in the Gospels[8] when he, James, and John went with Jesus to a mountaintop to pray. Jesus was transfigured (took on His glorified form) before their eyes and spoke with Moses and Elijah. Peter, being the impetuous man he was, said, "Let's build three tabernacles—one for You, one for Moses, and one for Elijah—to commemorate this amazing event!"

I love Peter. Sometimes he puts his foot in his mouth, but thank God for a guy who wants to do something! Here, he's a little misdirected, but God answers him from heaven, "No, we don't need to stop here and build, Peter. This is not the end. This is my beloved Son, listen to Him." Peter didn't realize it, but God was saying, "There are more important things coming, Peter; the cross is coming. Pay attention!"

At the transfiguration, Moses and Elijah appeared to talk with Jesus about the necessity of His suffering,[9] fulfilling all that was Written, and to remind Him of His future glory. Moses was there representing the Law, and Elijah the prophets, both of which pointed toward Christ. Peter saw all this with his eyes, but he argues:

> *We have also a more sure word of prophecy; to which you do well that you take heed, as unto a light that shines in a dark place, until the day dawns, and [The Power and Life of the Word] the day star arise in your hearts: Knowing this first, that no prophecy of the scripture is of any private interpretation. For the prophecy came not in old time by the will of man: but holy men of God spoke as they were moved by the Holy Spirit.*
>
> 2 Peter 1:19-21

Peter says, "We were with Jesus in the flesh. We witnessed His transfiguration and saw Him talking with Moses and Elijah. We heard God speaking from heaven, yet we have a 'more sure word of prophecy.'"

What was he talking about? You have to understand, they were working from Old Testament scriptures. They didn't have Matthew, Mark, Luke, and John. They didn't have Acts or Romans. They didn't have the New Testament as we know it, and yet he said, "We have a more sure word of prophecy." He is saying that the Old Testament prophesies of Christ's coming are greater cause for faith and certainty than actually seeing Christ in the flesh. He's saying that the Word of God is surer than something he experienced with his five senses.

We need to take that type of attitude toward the Word of God saying, "The Word of God is more real to me than if Jesus was here in the flesh! Even if I was among three of his closest followers, and saw Moses and Elijah, and heard God speak audibly from heaven, yet I would more readily believe the Word above all." If *we* determined to believe the Word like that, then the Word would produce a harvest in *our* lives, just like it did in the lives of the apostles.

Our attitude toward the Word reveals the place that God holds in our daily lives. It is a quick indicator of our relationship with Him. What are we doing with the Word? What do we believe about the Word? What place does it hold in our lives?

Is it our guiding principle, our final authority? Or is it just another book in our collection? What we find ourselves doing with the Word determines what the Word can do with us. The Bible tells us Heaven's attitude toward the Word. It says in Psalms,

> *Forever, O Lord, your word is settled in heaven.*
>   Psalm 119:89

> *The sum of thy word is truth; and every one of thy righteous ordinances endureth forever.*
>   Psalm 119:160 (ASV)

and in Isaiah,

> *So will My word be which goes forth from My mouth; It will not return to Me empty, without accomplishing what I desire, and without succeeding in the matter for which I sent it.*
>   Isaiah 55:11 (NASB)

As far as Heaven is concerned, the Word is an established fact. When God speaks a word, His Word goes out into eternity and produces fruit. It never quits bearing fruit. What God speaks is not only true but becomes Truth!

> *By the word of the Lord were the heavens made, their starry host by the breath of his mouth. For he spoke, and it came to be; he commanded, and it stood firm.*
>   Psalm 33:6, 9 (NIV)

> *God, who gives life to the dead, and calls those things which are not as though they were.*
>   Romans 4:17b

God's Word created the heavens and the earth. What He speaks creates and changes reality to conform to His Word. When He calls something that is not as though it was, the Word He spoke releases power to change the situation.

That verse in Romans 4 refers to how He renamed Abraham "father of many nations" even though Abraham was childless at the time.

Imagine introducing yourself for years as "father of many nations" when you don't even have one son! Many of us would be challenged by that, but Abraham didn't let it bother him. The Bible says "he believed" what the Lord had spoken.[10] He had respect for God's Word because he realized that what God says is true and has the ability to become Truth.

Of course, we know the end of the story: Abraham's faith in the grace of God enabled him and his wife to conceive. If we believe the Word above all else, as Abraham did, it will change the impossible situations we face. That is faith. That is having a good attitude toward the Word.

Do we take the Word of God as absolute truth? Do we honor the Word above everything else? God's Word **is true** but whether or not we believe it determines whether or not we can receive from it. When we adopt the attitude that God's Word is true, that it is established fact, and we determine in our hearts that we are going to believe it, we put ourselves in a place to receive from God and see the power and life of the Word come to pass in our lives!

---

[1] 1 John 1:1

[2] Psalm 138:2

[3] Hebrews 1:3; 2 Peter 3:5

[4] Psalm 19:7

[5] Isaiah 55:8-9

[6] Proverbs 14:12

[7] John 1:14

[8] Matthew 17:1-8; Mark 8:2-8; Luke 9:28-36

[9] Luke 9:31

[10] Romans 4:3

CHAPTER TWO

RECEIVING THE WORD WITH MEEKNESS

God has a special purpose and plan for your life. He has a good will and you're in it! And just like Jeremiah, the way for you to find it is through the "Word of the Lord." There are two forms of God's Word that we put to work in our lives.

On one hand, we have the *logos* Word of God. *Logos* is the Greek word for "written." We have the written Word of God, the Bible, available for our everyday use. God uses the Bible to show us His character and His covenant, to renew our minds to think like Him, and to encourage, direct, and correct us.

Have you ever been chastened or corrected by God? I have. According to Merriam-Webster, to chasten means to "correct, discipline and purify; to prune and refine; or to restrain and humble." The Bible tells us that God chastens or disciplines the children He loves.[1]

On occasion, I am rebuked plainly by the Lord, but I don't let that rebuke destroy my confidence. Hearing God's rebuke encourages me. It reminds me of our relationship. It lets me know that He still loves me, and that He is still interested in using me despite my failure.

We see in the Word that the man whom God corrects is blessed![2] When I say I've been rebuked by the Lord, what I mean is, God chastens me the same way He speaks to me, by His Word. Psalm 94 says,

> *Blessed is the man you discipline, O Lord, the man you teach from your law.*
>
> Psalm 94:12 (NIV)

For example, I might catch myself thinking or going in the wrong direction and God will immediately cause His Word to come to my mind. When I remember the Word, it causes me to repent and I change what I'm thinking or doing so I can start back in the right direction. I may not be sinning, I may have just chosen something outside of His best for me. I may be heading toward a distraction or hindrance, but God will redirect me. He will instruct me through His Word. That is chastisement. God uses His *logos* Word to instruct us and lead us in His way.[3]

We also have the *rhema* Word of God. *Rhema* is the Greek word for "spoken." It refers to those things God speaks to us directly, specifically; those unctions of the spirit that line up with the *logos* word. Remember in Jeremiah four, when the Lord came and spoke to Jeremiah, "Before I formed you in the belly I knew you and before you came forth out of the womb, I sanctified you and I ordained you a prophet to the nations."[4]

This was God's *rhema* word. God told Jeremiah, "I have a very specific purpose for you; I have a very specific plan for your life. Before you were born, I set you apart to be a prophet." He spoke a Word to Jeremiah that would direct the course of the rest of his life!

Whether God uses His *logos* or His *rhema* word to speak to us, it is how we respond to that Word that will determine what the Word can produce in our lives. The Word produces different things in different people because they respond differently to the Word. God does not force His Word or His will on us. He does not make it come to pass in our lives. We must respond to the Word in a positive way so that the Word can produce a positive harvest in our lives. We must learn to receive the Word with meekness.

Being meek is simply being teachable, it is a fruit of the Spirit.[5] Merriam-Webster defines it as "enduring injury [rebuke] with patience and not resentment." It is the ability to hear where we've missed it without getting defensive or angry. It is important to learn to cultivate this product of the Spirit, so that we can allow the Word to enlighten us and bring us to correction.

Psalm 119 states,

> *The entrance of your words gives light; it gives understanding unto the simple.*
>
> Psalm 119:130

The word "entrance," is the Hebrew word for a figurative opening (*pethach*) and could be translated as "revelation."[6] The Hebrew word *bin* translated here as "understanding" is a root word and seen often in the Old Testament as "discerning,"[7] "skill,"[8] "prudence"[9] or "perception."[10] So, this verse could be translated, "the revelation of Your Word enlightens, making the fool wise and discerning."

The Word of God has the ability to make fools wise, but we have to receive It with meekness. We cannot allow ourselves to be offended or angry when God's Word reveals where we've gone astray. We must listen to the Word and allow It to change our core beliefs and actions.

James says meekness looks like this:

Therefore put away all filthiness and extreme wickedness, and receive with meekness the engrafted word, which is able to save your souls. But be you doers of the word, and not hearers only, deceiving your own selves.

James 1:18, 21-22

The Word will save or transform our souls if we will receive It with meekness and become a "doer." Or you might say that the Word has the ability to produce the fruit of salvation, just like the Bible says, "Blessed be the Lord who daily loads me with benefits."[11]

It is similar to how a tree will produce fruit when we properly take care of it. It might take a tree a while to grow large enough to produce fruit, but if a tree is planted and watered, pruned and properly taken care of, eventually that tree will produce fruit.

My granddad planted an apricot tree on our property when he was a kid. He planted this tree in the early 1900s in an old canal. Eventually, they dug a new canal and drained the one the apricot was in. It never got enough water after that, but the tree would still produce a little here and there.

One winter we had so much snow that it drifted that old canal full! It was a cold winter, so the snow sat there for months. After spring melt, the tree blossomed and began to produce. As fall came closer, it looked like every limb was hanging to the ground full of fruit. That apricot tree was loaded to the max! We harvested all that fruit and Grandma made apricot jam. I think we ate jam for five years!

When Granddad's tree didn't get any water, it couldn't produce much fruit. It was a good tree, but it wasn't receiving what it needed to be productive. It's the same way with the Word; we must learn to water It with meekness. If we can't respond to the Word with a humble heart—if we don't change the way we think and act based on what It says— the Word won't be able to produce much fruit in our lives. God wants us to be like that old tree—loaded! If we learn to take a meek attitude toward the Word, we will see results.

The harvest off that tree was the natural result of water and seed, but Jesus said everything in the Kingdom works like this![12] The Word will produce a harvest. Harvest is the natural fruit of taking a meek attitude toward the Word.

Let's look back at James. In verse 21 he speaks of the "engrafted word." What's grafting talking about? Again, we can look at the natural example of trees. If you take an apple tree, say a Red Delicious, and graft a Granny Smith branch onto that tree you will produce both Red Delicious and Granny Smith apples on the same tree. You see, the life that is in the vine flows to the branch and causes it to bring forth fruit, regardless of the type of branch it is.

When we believed, we were grafted into God's covenant of blessing,[13] but unlike what happens with fruit trees, being attached to God's vine actually changes the fruit we produce. We can now produce the fruit of the covenant, which Galatians 5:22-23 defines as love, joy, peace, patience, kindness, goodness, faithfulness, gentleness, and self-control.

According to John 15, Jesus is the vine, and we are the branches. The life that is in Christ flows to us (if we abide in the Vine,[14]) and produces fruit. Notice that word, "abide." It means to stay. You can tell what someone's been meditating on, where they've been "staying," just by looking at their fruit. Jesus said, "by their fruit, you shall know them."[15] If you stay in Jesus and allow His Word to stay in you by receiving it with meekness, in the process of time, the life that's in the Word will produce fruit in your heart and you will see change in your situation!

In order to produce fruit and become a "doer of the Word" like James says, we must keep our minds "stayed" on the Vine and "desire the sincere milk of the Word." This constant supply of Word will help us mature.[16] Jesus said,

> *I tell you the truth, unless you change and become like little children, you will never enter the kingdom of heaven.*
>
> Matthew 18:3 (NIV)

Why do we have to enter the Kingdom as children? If there is one thing that can be said of all children, universally, it is that they are hungry: hungry for food but also hungry to learn. We need to have that same appetite for the Word, accepting it with a teachable heart in meekness.

The author of Hebrews says that the milk of the Word is one of the elementary, or foundational, principles of Christ including repentance and faith.[17] Once we have these basics down, once we stop trying to please God with our own goodness and believe what He said in His Word is true, we can go on to maturity. As long as we stay in the Word, not aborting the process with our own thoughts, eventually the Word will produce fruit. There is no way around it!

----

[1] Hebrews 12:5-6; Proverbs 3:11-12
[2] Psalm 94:12; Job 5:17
[3] Psalm 25:5, 43:3, 139:24
[4] Jeremiah 1:4-5
[5] Galatians 5:22-23
[6] Barnes' Notes on the Bible (1894) *Psalm 119*
[7] Genesis 41:33, 39; Deuteronomy 1:13; 1 Kings 3:9; Job 6:30; Proverbs 10:13
[8] 1 Chronicles 15:22, 25:7; 2 Chronicles 34:12
[9] Jeremiah 49:7; Isaiah 29:14, 10:13, 5:21; Proverbs 17:28, 18:15, 16:21; 1 Samuel 16:18
[10] Job 9:11, 14:21, 23:8, 38:18; 2 Samuel 12:19; Proverbs 1:2; Isaiah 6:9; Psalm 73:17
[11] Psalm 68:19
[12] Mark 4; Matthew 13; Luke 8
[13] Galatians 3:26; 4:5; John 1:12; Romans 10:4; Ephesians 2:11-22
[14] John 15:1-8
[15] Matthew 7:16
[16] 1 Peter 2:2
[17] Hebrews 6:1

CHAPTER THREE
USING WHAT WE HAVE

The *logos,* written, Word of God is powerful, like dynamite. Dynamite was used during the construction of Mount Rushmore. To begin carving these 60-foot sculptures in 1,200 acres of rock, workers would strap sticks of dynamite together into bundles, set a fuse, and get out of the way!

But what good would the dynamite have done without that fuse? The explosive material in dynamite is potent stuff, but without a fuse to light it, the dynamite is nearly worthless! Every written promise of God is like a stick of dynamite—phenomenal power potential—but the power it holds will sit unused without *rhema*!

Why? Because the *rhema,* spoken, Word of God produces faith within its hearers. When God speaks a Word, it is unmistakable! He may speak to us through the gifts of the Spirit (word of wisdom, word of knowledge, prophecy), He may speak to us through another person (preaching and teaching), or He may speak to our spirits and we simply have a peaceful "knowing" about a situation. But most often,

God speaks to us through His written Word.

Have you ever been reading the Word and something just jumps out to arrest your attention? You may have read that passage dozens of times, but for some reason this time was different. When the *logos* Word of God speaks directly to our situation and circumstance it becomes *rhema*, and we feel faith begin to rise up!

When the *logos* Word becomes *rhema* to us, it changes our lives! We need both the *logos* and the *rhema* Words of God to realize His plan and purpose for our lives. Just like dynamite, the power potential in the written Word of God must be lit with the fuse of our faith. A faith that is born by hearing the Word[1]—not just with our ears, but with the heart of faith.

As born-again believers we do not have a faith problem. The Word tells us every man has been given *the* measure of faith—even those who have yet to believe![2] We are believers: that's what we do. We believe in a God we cannot see. We believe in a place we've never been. We believe in a Savior we've never seen. We are believers!

A brief scripture study on faith will show you that you have the faith of Jesus Christ.[3] In fact, you have the same Spirit that raised Christ from the dead living in you,[4] and that Spirit is a Spirit of faith! There are not different measures of faith. I don't have "more faith" than you do. We are all—even Christ Himself—given the same measure of faith. Galatians tells us the natural fruit, or product, of the Spirit is faith.[5]

You might say, "Well ok, I have faith, but what do I do with it? How do I use it?" Let's look at this passage in Mark:

> *And one of the multitude answered and said,*
> *'Teacher, I have brought unto you my son, who*

has a dumb spirit; And wherever he takes him, he throws him down: and he foams, and gnashes with his teeth, and wastes away: and I spoke to your disciples that they should cast him out; and they could not.' He answered him, and said,' O faithless generation, how long shall I be with you? how long shall I bear with you? bring him unto Me.' And they brought him unto Him: and when He saw him, immediately the spirit convulsed him; and he fell on the ground, and wallowed foaming. And He asked his father, 'How long ago is it since this came unto him?' And he said, 'Since childhood. And often it has cast him into the fire, and into the waters, to destroy him: but if you can do anything, have compassion on us, and help us.'

Jesus said unto him, 'If you can believe, all things are possible to him that believes.' And immediately the father of the child cried out, and said with tears, 'Lord, I believe; help my unbelief.'

When Jesus saw that the people came running together, He rebuked the foul spirit, saying unto him, 'You dumb and deaf spirit, I charge you, come out of him, and enter no more into him.' And the spirit cried, and convulsed him terribly, and came out of him: and he was as one dead; so that many said, He is dead. But Jesus took him by the hand, and lifted him up; and he arose.

Mark 9:17-27

Here we see the father of a child with epilepsy who brings his son to Jesus for healing. Before going to Jesus, he approaches the disciples for prayer, but they didn't know how to deal with the problem.

Jesus answered, "Oh, faithless generation. Bring him to me." One translation calls them an "incredulous generation."[6] Incredulous means "unwilling to believe, full of doubt." The Word is not saying they don't *have* faith; it's saying they're having a problem *using* their faith.

When the disciples brought the boy to Jesus, "the spirit tare him and he fell on the ground, and wallowed foaming." The devil wanted to destroy that boy's life and his father's faith. He was using this manifestation to get everyone's attention and create fear.

He wants to destroy your life too. He wants to destroy your relationship with God. He wants you to doubt God's Word. Just as the devil used this family's circumstance to control their attention, the devil will use your circumstances to divert your focus from the Truth. We all possess faith, but the devil tries to distract and intimidate us to keep us from using what we have.

The devil came to destroy this young man; he was trying to kill him. The father spoke to Jesus, "If you can do anything, have compassion on us and help us." This man did not understand that God could, or that He would be willing to, help his family. He was so focused on the circumstance, he couldn't see beyond it to Christ's power and compassion. He said, "If you can..."

You know, most people believe that God *can*, but they don't know that He *will!* A lot of people say, "God, do something with this," but look how Jesus responded to the father: He turned the situation around and said, "If *you* can believe, all things are possible to him that believes."

"If you can believe." Jesus turned it around. The man came to the disciples, who couldn't help, and went to Jesus with the same expectation. "Jesus, *if* you can do something, please help me." Jesus said, "I want *you* to do something about the situation."

A lot of times, we say, "Lord, I brought my problem here, I brought my problem there, but nothing happened. What are You going to do?" But Jesus said, "I want *you* to do something." What did Jesus want him to do? He wanted him to believe. Jesus told the man, "If you can believe, all things are possible."

We have faith, but we must learn how to use what we have. How do we do that? The Word says, "Faith without works is dead."[7] That means we have to *do* something with what we truly believe. Someone once said, "Your faith must move you before it can move anything else!" But what does it move? It moves our tongues. Scripture says,

> *We having the same spirit of faith, according as it is written, I believed, and therefore have I spoken; we also believe, and therefore speak.*
>
> 2 Corinthians 4:13

> *…how can you, being evil, speak good things? For out of the abundance of the heart the mouth speaks.*
>
> Matthew 12:34

We speak what we believe. What we allow to come out of our mouths is a good indication of what we've been thinking about. The boy's father and the disciples had been focusing on the negative, looking and talking about the effects of the terrible disease the boy had. What do you spend most of your time talking about with co-workers, friends, and family? We must learn to get a hold of that thing between our teeth if we want to see the blessing of God flow freely in our lives. We need to line up our speaker with our believer!

Let's look again at Jeremiah. Jeremiah was called to be a prophet of God. God had a special plan for his life, but Jeremiah had to agree with God's plan if it was going to come to pass. God never forces His will or blessings on anyone! It is always our choice.[8]

> *Then the Word of the Lord came to me, saying, 'Before I formed thee in the belly I knew you; and before you came forth out of the womb I sanctified you, and ordained you a prophet to the nations.'*
>
> *Then I said, 'Ah Lord GOD! Behold, I cannot speak: for I am a child.' But the LORD answered me and said, 'Say not, I am a child: for you will go to all that I will send you, and whatever I command you, you shall speak. Do not afraid of their faces: for I am with you to deliver you,' says the LORD.*
>
> Jeremiah 1:4-8

God spoke with Jeremiah and revealed to him the purpose and plan for his life through His Word. (This is the same way He reveals our purpose to us.) But Jeremiah's response was not positive. He spoke words that directly contradicted what God said. "I can't do that," he replied, "I'm only a child!" Notice what God did. He immediately rebuked Jeremiah and said, "Do not say that!"

Has God ever spoken to you and said, "Don't say that!"? There is power and life in the Word of God, but there is also power in *our* words. God doesn't want us speaking words that are contrary to what He said. God understands the power (the spiritual nature) of words. We need to guard our words.

> *Death and life are in the power of the tongue: and they that love it shall eat the fruit of it.*
>
> Proverbs 18:21 (Webster)

Our words will either work for us or against us. The words we speak are a reflection of what is in our hearts. Jesus said, "Out of the abundance of the heart, the mouth speaketh."[9] He went on to say,

> *For by your words you shall be justified, and by your words you shall be condemned.*
>
> Matthew 12:37

By our words we can either enter into what God has provided, or we can miss out on His goodness.

Our words come from our dominant thoughts. That's why we have to guard what we think about. The words that we're speaking are a result of our focus. We can focus on the world and what the world says is fact (the problem) or we can choose to focus on what the Word says is true (the answer). We must learn to speak the answer not the problem! That's how we use our faith. That's how we light the fuse of the Word of God!

It is very important that we learn to speak the same words that God speaks. We need to say what He says, we need to agree.[10] We must determine to live by faith—by the conviction that what God says is True. We cannot live by what we only see with our eyes or feel with our hands. We must make up our minds to believe and speak the truth of God's Word. The Word that is spoken to us must be mixed with faith so that it can be spoken through us!

I've set my mind, and I am believing God right now for more than I've ever believed Him for in the past. And I'm beginning to see what I believe come to pass. Does that mean I never face challenges? No; we all have opportunities to use our faith. But whenever circumstances come against me saying "you can't," there must be something that rises up inside that says, "I can, in the Name of Jesus!"

Let us not be passive with our faith, let's use it and speak out what we believe.

One reason I believe our children have done so well is that we've never told them, "You can't do that." We brought them up saying, "If God is with you, you can do all things. Go for it."

Aaron, our oldest son, graduated from Carnegie Mellon University with honors. It was his number one choice of colleges, but when they sent the paperwork out and I saw how much it cost, I said, "Aaron, you are not going to that college." Aaron looked me straight in the face and said, "Dad, don't you believe God?" He preached my message back to me!

Andrew, our middle child, believed God too. Andrew said, "All of my college is going to be paid for." In fact, we found this little paper Andrew had folded up that said, "Do not read." Guess what? Mama found it, and she read it! Andrew had his life's goals written out on that paper. He wrote, "Number one: I'm going to serve God." That is a good goal. "Number two: I'm going to go to college and have it paid for. Number three: I'm going to get a good job making XXX money…" He continued listing good and godly goals (some of which seemed "out there"), but when we found that paper did we tell Andrew, "You can't do that." No, we encouraged him to believe God.

Andrew has accomplished several of those goals. One year at school he had eight different scholarships. The School of Mines contacted him and said, "You've got too much money. We have to take this scholarship away." Andrew replied, "That's okay; I'll get another one." Praise God! He completed his four-year degree in three years, graduating as the outstanding chemical engineering student –all paid for.

Peter, our youngest, decided when he was in seventh grade he was "going to get a full-ride scholarship." He went to Princeton University with tuition costs at $53,000 a year. How? Because Peter believed! Jesus said, "All things are possible if you can believe!"

Each of my boys had opportunity to use their faith. They took responsibility for what they believed and acted on it. You could see what they were believing by what they said and did. They were taking Jesus seriously when He said, "if you can believe."

It seems so easy for some to believe. Many people struggle in life because they've been taught not to believe; not to use their faith. When we talk about faith, the world thinks we're crazy. Even the church has told us we're unrealistic. They've been sold the lie that we can't change anything, but I'm here to tell you that God's reality—God's Word—is true regardless of man's experience or excuse,[11] and it can change your life!

To receive the promised blessings of God, we must pay attention to what we allow our minds to meditate on. We must watch what we speak out from our hearts. We must train ourselves to agree with God's Word and speak the answer not the problem! The Word of God that is spoken to us must be spoken through us! We're believers; let's believe!

[1] Romans 10:17
[2] Romans 12:3
[3] Galatians 2:16 (KJV)
[4] Romans 8:11
[5] Galatians 5:22
[6] Mark 9:22 (Douay-Rheims)
[7] James 2:26
[8] Deuteronomy 30:19
[9] Matthew 12:34
[10] Amos 3:3
[11] Romans 3:4

CHAPTER FOUR

DOUBT: THE ENEMY OF OUR FAITH

Scripture tells us that "faith comes by hearing and hearing by the Word of God."[1] When we hear God speak, when we hear the true Word of God declared—the Word He spoke about Himself and about us—our faith is lit and it will speak!

> *We having the same spirit of faith, according as it is written, I believed, and therefore have I spoken; we also believe, and therefore speak.*
>
> 2 Corinthians 4:13

But sometimes it seems we struggle receiving the promises of God. We know we have faith; we're believers, we have "the same spirit of faith." Not only do we have it, we're using it by speaking the truth. What's the problem? Do we need more faith? No. We don't have a faith problem, we have an unbelief problem.

James says, a "double-minded man [a man who goes from doubt to belief, doubt to belief] is unstable in all his ways." He says such a man cannot "receive anything from the Lord."[2] Look with me again at Mark chapter nine:

And one of the multitude answered and said, 'Teacher, I have brought unto you my son, who has a dumb spirit; And wherever he takes him, he throws him down: and he foams, and gnashes with his teeth, and wastes away: and I spoke to your disciples that they should cast him out; and they could not.' He answered him, and said,' O faithless generation, how long shall I be with you? how long shall I bear with you? bring him unto Me.'

And they brought him unto Him: and when He saw him, immediately the spirit convulsed him; and he fell on the ground, and wallowed foaming. And He asked his father, 'How long ago is it since this came unto him?' And he said, 'Since childhood. And often it has cast him into the fire, and into the waters, to destroy him: but if you can do anything, have compassion on us, and help us.'

Jesus said unto him, 'If you can believe, all things are possible to him that believes.' And immediately the father of the child cried out, and said with tears, 'Lord, I believe; help my unbelief.'

When Jesus saw that the people came running together, He rebuked the foul spirit, saying unto him, 'You dumb and deaf spirit, I charge you, come out of him, and enter no more into him.' And the spirit cried, and convulsed him terribly, and came out of him: and he was as one dead; so that many said, He is dead.

But Jesus took him by the hand, and lifted him up; and he arose. And when He was come into the house, His disciples asked Him privately, 'Why could not we cast him out?' And He said unto them, 'This kind can come forth by nothing, but by prayer and fasting.'

Mark 9:17-29

Notice the father's plea, "Lord, I believe. Help my unbelief." It is possible to believe something and yet still struggle with doubt. We must overcome unbelief if we are to enter into the blessing and plan God has for us.

Notice too, the disciples' reaction. "Why couldn't we cast it out?" They knew the power of Christ, they saw it every day. They knew He had given them power[3] over Satan and had even operated in that power to an extent,[4] so why was this circumstance different? Jesus said, "This kind can come out only by prayer and fasting."

What was Jesus talking about? Let me ask you a question. Does prayer and fasting change the devil? No. Does it change God? No. Then what is the purpose of prayer and fasting? Prayer and fasting changes you; it changes me. The challenge is not God—He made a promise and will keep it.[5] The challenge is not the devil—Christ was sent and destroyed the devil's power.[6] There aren't special devils that need extra prayer and fasting. The challenge is us. The challenge is our unbelief. Prayer and fasting helps us get rid of our unbelief.

Our flesh—our senses—speak to us very well. We've been training them for years to tell us how we feel, what we see, whether or not we're hungry, and on and on. The purpose of prayer and fasting is to get our flesh under control because our senses are a big source of unbelief.

The disciples' eyes and ears were speaking to them loudly that this young boy had a major problem, and it wasn't getting better. If we are constantly listening to our natural senses, how can we hear God; how can we act in faith? Faith's very definition is:

> ...the substance of things hoped for, the evidence of things not seen.
>
> Hebrews 11:1

If we are to act and speak in faith (on something we can't see) how can we focus on only those things we can see? Prayer and fasting doesn't affect the devil one bit. It doesn't affect demons one bit. It doesn't affect God either. Prayer and fasting affects us. In this passage, Jesus was giving us a strategy to overcome unbelief.

Let's look in greater detail about how to fight unbelief. First, we have to know where it comes from so we can learn to recognize it. Unbelief can come from several sources. One way it comes is through lack of knowledge. The Bible says:

> My people are destroyed for lack of knowledge.
>
> Hosea 4:6

> My people are gone into captivity because they have no knowledge.
>
> Isaiah 5:13

What you don't know can hurt you! It's important what we know. In fact, the Bible says, "Faith comes by hearing and hearing by the Word of God."[7] Or we could look at the literal Greek, "Faith comes by declaration and declaration by the mouth of God." Faith comes when someone declares to us who God said that He is.

God said, "I am the Lord, your provider. I am the Lord, your healer. I am the Lord, your peace. I am the Lord, your deliverer. I am the Lord, your sanctification. I am the Lord, your righteousness. I am the Lord who is there."[8] If we don't know who God is, if we don't know what He has provided for us, it can hinder us from receiving and fulfilling all that God has planned for our lives. Not knowing who God is and what He has to say about your situation is a major source of unbelief.

Another way unbelief comes is by the traditions of men. Let's look at Mark 7:13 in a variety of translations:

> *Making the word of God of none effect through your tradition... (KJV)*

> *And so you cancel the word of God in order to hand down your own tradition...   (NLT)*

> *Thus invalidating the word of God by your tradition… (NASB)*

> *You are destroying the word of God through your tradition… (ISV)*

> *And you reject the word of God for the traditions that you deliver… (Aramaic NT)*

> *Because of your traditions you have destroyed the authority of God's word... (God's Word)*

Some of us attend churches that preach "maybe God will, maybe God won't; you don't ever know about God." What a beautiful 'gospel' for excusing the failures of man! The way most churches preach the 'sovereignty of God' only makes people feel good; it doesn't encourage them to grow.

They say, "If you receive, God is good! If you don't, God is teaching you an important lesson. Be happy, both are under God's control." That is a lie! It's nothing more than a tradition or doctrine of man that undermines what God's Word says.

You know why they tell you that? To avoid responsibility. The teaching of faith—the true Word of God—will challenge you; it will make you grow and mature. When I first heard the Word of God preached, I thought, "Praise God! I don't have to sit on my blessed assurance and hope for someone or something to come down the pipe to make my life better. I can believe God!" I began to take responsibility for what was happening in my life. Without that revelation from the Word, we get stuck in traditions that are full of unbelief.

The final way unbelief comes is through circumstances. Doubt often tries to raise its ugly head when we have made a decision to believe God. That was what was the disciples were dealing with in Mark chapter nine. What happened when the father brought his son to Jesus? As soon as Jesus speaks the Word, "you foul spirit, come out of him," the boy falls over and starts wallowing and foaming and rolling in the dirt!

Jesus had spoken a word, and immediately a source of doubt and fear showed up. The circumstances were very negative, and it produced unbelief in the disciples. They had good teaching, they knew it was God's will for the boy to be healed, and yet the situation intimidated them. The circumstances became more real than God's Word.

My dad had epilepsy; when he'd have an attack, it was ugly. He'd fall down in the street and roll around. It bothered people who didn't understand what was going on. It put them in fear. The devil was trying to do that very thing in Mark nine. He was trying to grip the father and the disciples with fear.

He's trying to intimidate you, too. He's using your circumstances to eliminate your faith, to make you doubt the truth of God's Word. But hang on! It is just circumstantial evidence. Just like in a court of law, circumstantial evidence has no authority, no weight. Don't allow that tactic to win!

Let's look at another example in Matthew:

> *And immediately Jesus made his disciples get into a ship, and to go before Him unto the other side, while He sent the multitudes away. And when He had sent the multitudes away, He went up into a mountain apart to pray: and when the evening was come, He was there alone. But the ship was now in the midst of the sea, tossed with waves: for the wind was contrary.*
>
> *And in the fourth watch of the night Jesus went unto them, walking on the sea. And when the disciples saw Him walking on the sea, they were troubled, saying, 'It is a spirit;' and they cried out for fear. But immediately Jesus spoke unto them, saying, 'Be of good cheer; it is I; be not afraid.'*
>
> *And Peter answered Him and said, 'Lord, if it be You, bid me come unto You on the water.' And He said, 'Come.' And when Peter came down out of the ship, he walked on the water, to go to Jesus. But when he saw the wind boisterous, he was afraid; and beginning to sink, he cried, saying, 'Lord, save me.' And immediately Jesus stretched forth his hand, and caught him, and said unto him, 'O you of little faith, why did you doubt?' And when they came into the ship, the wind ceased. Then they that were in the ship came and worshiped Him, saying, 'Of a truth You are the Son of God.'*
>
> Matthew 14:22-33

After feeding the multitude, Jesus put his disciples in the boat and told them to go to the other side of the lake. During their sail, a storm arose. This happens often on the Sea of

Galilee, and the disciples were using all their experience to get to the other side in one piece; they were focused on fulfilling the directive of Jesus. Along comes Jesus, walking on the water. Scripture says He would have passed by them and met them on the shore, but the disciples cried out. Peter said, "Lord, if it's you, tell me to come." Jesus said, "Come."

There was enough power in that one Word for every one of the disciples to get out of the boat and walk on the water! But only Peter got out. A lot of people criticize Peter. When he saw the wind blowing and the waves raging, he began to sink, but at least he got out of the boat! At least he tried using his faith!

Peter fell into the same trap we all do; he saw the circumstances. He took his eyes off Jesus and fear immediately drained his faith. As he began to sink, Jesus reached out His hand, picked him up, and walked with him back to the boat. Thank God for people who try to use their faith! Don't criticize somebody for believing God. Don't criticize someone for getting out of the boat and falling.

If you've gotten out of the boat, praise God! Keep your eyes on Jesus; keep your eyes on His Word. Keep walking. If you fall down, get back up again. Keep believing God! Keep moving forward in your faith. Circumstances will come and try to drain your faith, but keep walking! Jesus said we can pray and fast to help keep our flesh under control and see past the problem to the answer. It helps us kill the unbelief and see with eyes of faith!

When you are challenged, you can look in the mirror of the Word and see what the Word says about you, or you can look in the mirror of circumstances and see what the circumstances say. It's your choice. Are you going to believe what God said about you? Are you going to believe what

God said about Himself? Or are you going to believe what the world says or what the circumstances are telling you? You've got to make a choice.

There is not a problem with our faith. We have faith, and once we get out of the boat—once we start acting like what God said is true—we're using it. The challenge is not with our faith; the challenge is with unbelief. We need to agree with the Lord, with His Word. We need to say what God says, and see what God sees. We need to agree with God so that we can begin to experience what God has promised in His Word. We have to pull the plug on unbelief!

---

[1] Romans 10:17
[2] James 1:7-8
[3] Luke 9:1
[4] Luke 10:17
[5] Psalm 105:8
[6] 1 John 3:8
[7] Romans 10:17
[8] Genesis 22:14; Exodus 15:26; Judges 6:24; Exodus 17:15; Leviticus 20:8; Jeremiah 23:6; Ezekiel 48:35

PART TWO

RENEWING OUR MINDS

And be renewed in the spirit of your mind…
Ephesians 4:23

CHAPTER FIVE

SEEING THINGS FROM GOD'S PERSPECTIVE

To truly experience God's best, as shown to us in His Word, we need to begin to see things from His perspective. The Word says,

> *Seek the Lord while he may be found; call on him while he is near. Let the wicked forsake his way and the evil man his thoughts. Let him turn to the Lord, and he will have mercy on him, and to our God, for he will freely pardon. For as the heavens are higher than the earth, so are my ways higher than your ways, and my thoughts than your thoughts.*

> Isaiah 55:6-9

We don't naturally think like God. Nearly all of the major principles in the Word are completely opposite of the world's system.

Scripture lays out principles such as: "love your enemy,"[1] "give and it will be given to you,"[2] "pride comes before a fall,"[3] and "even a fool is thought wise who holds his tongue."[4]

But the world says "take care of number one," "get what you can, and can all you get," "you get what you deserve," and "bigger is always better." The natural man's thoughts are completely upside-down! If we want our lives to be transformed, we have to begin to see things from God's perspective. Paul tells us:

> *And be not conformed to this world: but be transformed by the renewing of your mind, that you may prove what is that good, and acceptable, and perfect, will of God.*
>
> Romans 12:2

For years I looked at this scripture and thought that "renewing your mind" meant reading and memorizing scripture so I could cram my brain with as many Biblical facts as possible and push out all my unholy thoughts. But that is not true mind renewal.

Ephesians says to be "renewed in the spirit (or attitude) of your mind."[5] Mind renewal is an attitude adjustment; it is a retraining. True mind renewal is purposefully choosing to see things from God's perspective.

Does memorizing scripture help? Absolutely. Is reading the Word essential? Yes. But we aren't reading simply to gather information or memorize facts, we're reading to discover God's character, His promises, and His view of us. We're choosing not to think like the world, but to "think on these things:"

> *Finally, brethren, whatsoever things are true, whatsoever things are honest, whatsoever things are just, whatsoever things are pure, whatsoever things are lovely, whatsoever things are of good report; if there be any virtue, and if there be any praise, think on these things.*
>
> Philippians 4:8

Why does God tell us to think about those things? Because that's what He thinks about! Mind renewal is all about thinking like God. Even though His thoughts are higher than ours like Isaiah says,[6] we can learn to think like Him.

Remember Jeremiah? God had to teach him this same principle. He had to teach Jeremiah to think on "whatsoever things are true;" to think on His Word and consider *His* Word as the final authority.

> *Then the word of the LORD came unto me, saying, 'Before I formed you in the womb I knew you; and before you came forth out of the womb I sanctified you, and I ordained you a prophet unto the nations.' Then said 'I, Ah, Lord GOD! behold, I cannot speak: for I am a child.'*
>
> *But the LORD said unto me, 'Say not, I am a child: for you shall go to all that I shall send you, and whatsoever I command you you shall speak. Be not afraid of their faces: for I am with you to deliver you,' says the LORD.*
>
> *Then the Lord put forth his hand, and touched my mouth. And the LORD said unto me, 'Behold, I have put my words in your mouth. See, I have this day set you over the nations and over the kingdoms, to root out, and to pull down, and to destroy, and to throw down, to build, and to plant.'*
>
> *Moreover the word of the LORD came unto me, saying, Jeremiah, 'What seest thou?' And I said, 'I see a rod of an almond tree'. Then said the LORD unto me, 'Thou hast well seen: for I will hasten my word to perform it.'*

Jeremiah 1:4-12

When the Lord came and spoke to Jeremiah, Jeremiah's response was not positive. He did not see things the way the Lord did. "I cannot speak," he said, "I am a child." But the Lord rebuked him, "Jeremiah, don't say that!" Jeremiah's words were revealing his perspective about himself. The Lord was calling him to be a prophet, but Jeremiah didn't see how that could be possible.

God understands how our perspective and the things that we say influence our lives. He was trying to alter Jeremiah's view of himself. We must begin to see ourselves the way God sees us if we are going to experience the things God has planned for us.

A lot of people are like Jeremiah and don't yet see things through God's eyes. This often hinders them from receiving the promises of God. Jeremiah's idea of himself was natural, completely contrary to God's. During their conversation, God interrupted Jeremiah to remind him who he was *created* to be, who God saw him to be. "Jeremiah," He said, "I have a plan for you. Don't be afraid, I'll be with you. I've made you a prophet to these people." The Lord corrected Jeremiah's perception and began the work of retraining his brain. He wants to do the same thing for us.

When our minds are renewed, it affects what we see. God asked Jeremiah, "What do you see?" God needed Jeremiah to change the picture he saw on the inside of himself. He wanted him to realize that when God calls, He also equips.[7] Jeremiah didn't see himself as capable of doing what God called him to do. Without changing that perspective, Jeremiah would have never been able to accomplish what God had planned for his life.

Jeremiah replied, "I see a rod of an almond tree." Now, almond trees are native to Palestine and Syria. They are unique trees. Almonds bloom in the middle of winter before they get any leaves. When the tree looks absolutely lifeless, it shoots into bloom. This is a picture of the Word of God.

When God speaks a Word, regardless of whether it looks like there is anything happening, that Word will work until it accomplishes what it was sent to do![8] God told Jeremiah that He'd created him a prophet. Jeremiah didn't understand how that was possible; he didn't see the fruit of a prophet in his life, but God spoke a Word. And when God speaks, His Word produces life!

God praised Jeremiah for seeing accurately. "You have well seen," He told Jeremiah, "for I will hasten My Word to perform it." Just like the almond hastens to produce fruit, one Word from God can change a lifeless situation because God always looks after His Word! If we want to experience a different dimension of blessing, then we must begin to see ourselves clearly—through the Word—so that it can change the picture on the inside of us.

My parents went to school in Pueblo, Colorado. My dad had epilepsy and couldn't get steady work, so my mom was the family's "bread-winner." We lived in a 10' by 60' trailer house that cost $600. My parents drove an old Ford station wagon with over 200,000 miles on it; they just barely got by. We would burn coal in our house for heat because it was cheap—it stunk, and it burnt our eyes. But that's where we came from.

When my family heard the true Word of God preached, that old picture began to change. I told my dad, "When I'm an adult, I'm going to have enough money to buy natural gas." Something just went off in me, I decided to believe God! You know, statistically speaking, most people will never go beyond where their parents lived. Most people will never get a better education, drive a better car, or live in a better house than their parents. Why? Because that's the way they see life. But if you can break that picture, you can change that experience. The Word of God has the power to change our internal picture just like it changed Jeremiah's.

We have to believe what God says about us so that we can begin to experience what God says belongs to His children. That's why I don't just preach what I've experienced. Thank God, I've experienced good things in my life. Thank God, the Word is coming to pass, but I'm not only preaching what I've experienced, because I don't want you to be limited to what I've experienced.

There is power and life in the Word, and I want you to experience the promises God has given in His Word! I will preach the Word. I will never abandon it. I know it is the Word of God that brings life. You see, if we can change our picture on the inside, then the picture on the outside will change too.

Let's look at the parable of the sower in Mark chapter four. Jesus said that everything in the Kingdom operates according to the parable of the sower.[9] Notice verse 24 and 25:

> *And he said unto them, 'Take heed what you hear: with what measure you measure, it shall be measured to you: and unto you that hear shall more be given. For he that has, to him shall be given: and he that has not, from him shall be taken even that which he has.*

Mark 4:24-25

Jesus said, "Pay attention to what you hear, what you allow to enter your thought process. Guard your mind." He went on to say, "For the one that has will be given more; and the one that doesn't, will lose even what he has."

Some people read that scripture and say it's a confirmation of what Job said, "The Lord gives and the Lord takes away."[10] That is not what this scripture is saying. If we compare it with the parable of the talents in Matthew 25, we'll see that the person who uses what they've been given, receives more. And the person who doesn't, even what they had is taken (notice it does not say by God) and given to someone who will use it. Stewardship always leads to increase; it is a natural law, like the law of gravity.

But notice the earlier part, Jesus said, "Pay attention to what you allow your mind to digest." Begin to believe the things God has spoken over you. What we think about—and how we think about it—determines what we say and ultimately what we do.[11] What you decide to do with the Word determines what the Word can do with you.

God has a special plan for *your* life. It may not look like your neighbor's plan, or your mother's plan. It probably won't look like your pew buddy's plan either, but it is a good plan that needs your cooperation.

How do we cooperate? By being careful to what and whom we listen, by purposefully digesting the Word of God. There are lots of negative people with negative news that will not help us move forward in life. Our hearts must be full of the Word—full of what God says and thinks—in order for us to accomplish God's plan.

When everyone in the world is prospering, it's hard to tell the difference between God's people and those who operate by merely natural processes. But when all hell breaks loose in the world and natural or financial disasters happen, you can tell whether or not God's people have been meditating on His Word—their expectations and results are different. They just see things differently.

God called Barbara and I to start a church in Colorado Springs, in 2001. Our very first Sunday service was held on September 10, 2001, a day before the terrorist attack on the Twin Towers. Most people look at that and think, "It's a bad time to start a church, a bad time to start anything." But the Word makes you see things differently; it changes the picture on your inside. We just kept our eyes on Jesus, remembered His Word to us, and kept moving forward. We refused to stop doing what God told us to do just because the world was going crazy.

John G. Lake went to South Africa years ago. During that time thousands of people were dying of the plague, but he wasn't afraid. People were questioning his sanity in the midst of all that turmoil, but he continued to pray for the sick, visit them, and tell them about the power of God.

One day, Lake was in a medical clinic and the doctors there showed him germs from a person suffering with the plague under a microscope. He told one of the patients, "Spit on me." Then he took a slide and rubbed it over his body where he was spit upon. When the doctors looked at it under a microscope, every one of the germs were dead! Lake said, "I've got so much of the anointing, so much of the life of God in me, that disease cannot live in my body."

How was Lake able to do this? He had "retrained" his mind. The picture on his inside was lining up with what God said was true. Lake spent so much time with the Word that the Word had become a part of him. He had digested the Truth to the point that it was reproducing itself in his body.

The Word will always bring forth fruit! This "mind digestion" is the second step in receiving from God. First, you must believe and begin to see things as God does, then, you must conceive like Psalm talks about:

Blessed is the man that walks not in the counsel of the ungodly, nor stands in the way of sinners, nor sits in the seat of the scornful. But his delight is in the law of the LORD; and in his law does he meditate day and night. And he shall be like a tree planted by the rivers of water, that brings forth its fruit in its season; his leaf also shall not wither; and whatsoever he does shall prosper.

Psalm 1:1-3

The psalmist says to "meditate day and night" on the law or Word of God. The Hebrew word here "to meditate" is *hagah,* which means to "utter, to mutter, to meditate, to devise, to imagine, to speak, to roar!" The concept here is to put God's Word constantly before your eyes and in your mind,[12] to digest it. This is the conception process—when what we meditate on becomes what we see. When we take the time to conceive the Word, Jeremiah says:

For he shall be as a tree planted by the waters, and that spreads out its roots by the river, and shall not fear when the heat comes, but its leaf shall be green; and shall not be anxious in the year of drought, neither shall cease from yielding fruit.

Jeremiah 17:8

Let's look again at Psalm one. Remember the Hebrew word for meditate is *hagah.* Look at the progression of that word "utter, mutter, meditate, devise, imagine, speak, roar." Spiritually, when we begin to digest and conceive the Word, we "utter" or speak it as in reading, we "meditate" or think on it, we "imagine" it by picturing within ourselves what it would be like to see God's promise come to pass. We "speak" it, for what we believe will naturally rise up within us, and we "roar!"

What happens when a lion roars? Everyone in the jungle knows he is there! When we roar, the picture inside of us is refusing to keep silent, it is refusing to be held back; our faith is making itself known! God is "hastening to perform His Word." Conception is "speeding up" the process of our receiving. Look at 2 Corinthians 1:

> *For no matter how many promises God has made, they are "Yes" in Christ. And so through him the "Amen" is spoken **by us** to the glory of God.*
>
> 2 Corinthians 1:20 (NIV; emphasis mine)

God shouted, "Yes," at the cross! When Christ took our infirmities and sin upon Himself and the new covenant was enacted by God, when Christ rose from the dead defeating Satan, all the promises of that new covenant were deposited in our account! The grace of God has provided forgiveness, righteousness, healing, peace, provision, and protection for us. But we have to answer God's divine "YES" with our own "Amen" of faith; we have to agree with God.

That doesn't just mean being able to quote the scriptures. Our thinking and our perception has to line up with how God sees things. The greatest barrier of our faith happens within our own minds. Let's make our focus the Word. Let's meditate on the Word and allow it to change what we see!

---

[1] Matthew 5:44
[2] Luke 6:38
[3] Proverbs 16:18
[4] Proverbs 17:28
[5] Ephesians 4:23
[6] Isaiah 55:8
[7] Philippians 2:13, Hebrews 13:21 (NLT)
[8] Isaiah 55:11
[9] Mark 4:11
[10] Job 1:21
[11] Matthew 12:35
[12] Joshua 1:8

Chapter Six

The Word is Seed

The Word has the power to change our lives, but it must first change our minds. Ephesians 4:23 says to "be renewed in the spirit of our mind." Let's look in greater depth at what that actually means. First, we need to understand that the Word is seed.

In the kingdom of God, everything—even spiritual principles—works according to the principle of the seed and the sower.[11] Someone once asked Smith Wigglesworth, "How does great faith come?" Quoting Mark 4:28, Smith said, "First the blade, then the ear, then the full corn in the ear."

How does a physical seed grow? In the same way, you plant a seed and soon a blade pops up through the ground. In a bit, you see an ear (the head or bloom, depending on the plant). Later, the full corn appears. The seed is producing fruit.

Every time you plant a garden you are living out a picture of the miracle-working power of seed. The nature of seed is reproduction—fruit. Inside every seed is an exact copy of its species that will grow and produce thousands of additional seeds *exactly like the first*. It replicates itself.

You cannot plant corn seed and expect to get green beans, or plant watermelons and yet become angry when the harvest doesn't provide you with pumpkins. Anyone who planted pine nuts in a window box would be considered insane! The nature of seed, no matter what variety, is to "produce after its own kind."[2]

Jesus told a parable:

> *'A sower went out to sow his seed: and as he sowed, some fell by the wayside; and it was trodden down, and the fowls of the air devoured it. And some fell upon a rock; and as soon as it was sprung up, it withered away, because it lacked moisture. And some fell among thorns; and the thorns sprang up with it, and choked it. And other fell on good ground, and sprang up, and bore fruit a hundredfold. And when he had said these things, he cried, 'He that has ears to hear, let him hear.'*
>
> *And his disciples asked him, saying, "'What might this parable be?'…*
>
> *'Now the parable is this: The seed is the word of God. Those by the wayside are they that hear; then comes the devil, and takes away the word out of their hearts, lest they should believe and be saved. Those on the rock are they, who, when they hear, receive the word with joy; and these have no root, who for awhile believe, and in time of temptation fall away. And that which fell among thorns are they, who, when they have heard, go forth, and are choked with cares and*

*riches and pleasures of this life, and bring no fruit
to maturity. But that on the good ground are they,
who in an honest and good heart, having heard
the word, keep it, and bring forth fruit with
patience.'*

Luke 8:5-9, 11-15

In this story, a farmer went out to sow his seed. He expected the seed to do its job, conforming to its nature by reproducing, but when harvest came, the farmer returned with very mixed results! Some seed landed on the road and was lost. Some seed fell among the rocks, where it sprouted but withered quickly for a lack of soil. Some seed was sown among the weeds; there it grew up but was soon choked out because of the high demands of the weeds. And still some seed fell in good soil where it could produce a harvest.

Notice that all of the seed "sprang up," but it produced differently—some thirty, sixty, and hundred-fold what was sown.[3] It is obvious in Jesus' parable that the seed wasn't at fault. The variable was the ground. Jesus explained that it was the condition of the ground that determined the result of the seed, but the seed always worked according to its nature.

Jesus also said the kingdom of God works by this same principle.[4] The seed is the Word. Like all seed, there is not a problem with the Word. It will produce a harvest, but we must allow it to do its work.

*And He said, 'So is the kingdom of God, as if a
man should cast seed into the ground; And
should sleep, and rise night and day, and the
seed should spring and grow up, he knows not
how. For the earth brings forth fruit of itself; first
the blade, then the ear, after that the full grain in
the ear. But when the fruit is brought forth,*

> *immediately he puts in the sickle, because the harvest is come.'*

Mark 4:26-28

If you planted seed, you would never go out and dig it up saying, "It's not working. It looks just like it did yesterday." When a farmer plants a seed, he leaves it and goes about his business. He may drive by every day and see nothing, but the farmer knows the seed he planted will produce according to its nature. That is faith: believing in that which you cannot see. One day, while driving by, the farmer notices the seed has begun to sprout; it is working, "for the earth yields crops by itself." The seed works—the Word works! The only variable is the soil, which is the heart—your heart.[5]

Your heart is just like a garden, it is bringing forth a harvest of whatever seed has been planted in it. If you don't like your harvest, first check your seed. Are you planting weeds or the Word? Remember, seed will produce after its kind. Next check your ground. Just like a farmer can improve and adjust the soil with fertilizers and compost, you have the ability to change your heart.

What we meditate on determines, to great extent, the condition of our hearts. Jesus told us to "take heed what [we] hear."[6] What we allow our minds to digest is important. The things we think about have great influence in our hearts and on our attitudes. What we choose to meditate on can change the soil of our hearts.

Proverbs says,

> *Keep your heart with all diligence; for out of it are the issues of life.*

Proverbs 4:23

The New Living translation says it like this:

Guard your heart above all else, for it determines the course of your life.

Proverbs 4:23

Let's look at an example of two brothers, who, growing up in the same house—with the same parents and the same surroundings—got very different results.

Jacob and Esau:

And the LORD said unto her, 'Two nations are in your womb, and two manner of people shall be born of you; and the one people shall be stronger than the other people; and the elder shall serve the younger.' And when her days to be delivered were fulfilled, behold, there were twins in her womb. And the first came out red, all over like a hairy garment; and they called his name Esau. And after that came his brother out, and his hand took hold on Esau's heel; and his name was called Jacob: and Isaac was three score years old when she bore them. And the boys grew: and Esau was a skillful hunter, a man of the field; and Jacob was a quiet man, dwelling in tents. And Isaac loved Esau, because he did eat of his venison: but Rebekah loved Jacob.

And Jacob boiled pottage: and Esau came from the field, and he was faint: And Esau said to Jacob, 'Feed me, I pray you, with that same red pottage; for I am faint:' therefore was his name called Edom. And Jacob said,' Sell me this day your birthright.' And Esau said, 'Behold, I am at the point of death: and what profit shall this birthright be to me?' And Jacob said, 'Swear to me this day;' and he swore unto him: and he sold his birthright unto Jacob. Then Jacob gave Esau bread and pottage of lentils; and he did eat and drink, and rose up, and went his way: thus Esau despised his birthright.

Genesis 25:23-34

Jacob and Esau grew up in the same house, but the soil of their hearts was different. Esau despised his birthright, while Jacob valued it enough to go after it. Someone might say, "But that's just personality differences. You can't blame their lives on the condition of their hearts. Besides, Jacob later lied to his father to steal the blessing."

Let's read further:

*And Rebekah heard when Isaac spoke to Esau his son. And Esau went to the field to hunt for venison, and to bring it. And Rebekah spoke unto Jacob her son, saying, 'Behold, I heard your father speak unto Esau your brother, saying, Bring me venison, and make me savory food, that I may eat, and bless you before the LORD before my death. Now therefore, my son, **obey my voice** according to that which I command you. Go now to the flock, and fetch me from there two good kids of the goats; and I will make them savory food for your father, such as he loves: And you shall bring it to your father, that he may eat, and that he may bless you before his death.'*

*And Jacob said to Rebekah his mother, 'Behold, Esau my brother is a hairy man, and I am a smooth man: My father perhaps will feel me, and I shall seem to him as a deceiver; and I shall bring a curse upon me, and not a blessing.' And his mother said unto him, 'Upon me be your curse, my son: only **obey my voice**, and go bring me them.' And he went, and took, and*

brought them to his mother: and his mother made savory food, such as his father loved.
                    Genesis 27:5-14 (emphasis mine)

Was Jacob's act one that came from his own heart, or that of his mother's? We can see another example of the boys' heart differences if we continue reading:

*When Esau saw that Isaac had blessed Jacob, and sent him away to Paddanaram, to take him a wife from there; and that as he blessed him he gave him a charge, saying, 'You shall not take a wife of the daughters of Canaan;' And that **Jacob obeyed his father and his mother**, and was gone to Paddanaram; And Esau seeing that the daughters of Canaan pleased not Isaac his father; Then went Esau unto Ishmael, and took, **besides the wives whom he had**, Mahalath the daughter of Ishmael Abraham's son, the sister of Nebaioth, to be his wife.*
                    Genesis 28:6-9 (emphasis mine)

It is obvious in these passages that Jacob honored his parents—thus honoring God—and obeyed what they asked of him. It seems apparent that Esau took his position in the family for granted. He did not honor his parents or listen to their counsel. When he did "obey" it was with selfish motives; he tried to "win back" the blessing of his father by finally choosing to heed his words and marry a woman of their tribe. Ultimately, this heart difference promoted Jacob and gave him a permanent place in the fatherhood of God's people.[7] The condition of his heart allowed the seed of God's Word to produce a harvest in his life.

Seed always produces according to its nature, but harvest is determined by the soil. The Word of God is just like a seed. It is alive and has the power to produce life, but the quality of our soil, the condition of our hearts, will determine the amount of our harvest.

Just like in Jesus' parable, the seed from the Word has been scattered or released countless times, yet there are a lot of people who have not produced harvest from the Word. What has happened? Either their "soil" was not prepared for the seed, as Jesus said, or they have heard the Word but not mixed it with faith.

Just like in natural birth, when seed leaves a man's body, it joins an egg and is planted in a woman's womb. Before one of those seeds can bring forth a child there must be a conception process. In spiritual principles, this conception happens when we mix our faith with the Grace of God's Word and believe.

The Word works: like seed it will produce a harvest! But we have the power to determine the amount of our harvest. Our soil—our heart—is the variable. We must meditate on the things of God and prepare our hearts to receive His Word. When we do, we can be assured that the Word will work for us!

---

[1] Matthew 13:11
[2] Genesis 1:11
[3] Matthew 13:8
[4] Matthew 13:11
[5] Matthew 13:19
[6] Mark 4:24
[7] Genesis 32:28-29

Chapter Seven
The Conception Period

When God wants to accomplish something in your life, He speaks His Word. The Word is life! Scripture tells us "He calls those things that be not as though they were."[1] God can create life from a dead or impossible situation with just one Word! But before we can see the life of that Word take over, we must conceive it. Let's look at an example in Luke.

> *And in the sixth month the angel Gabriel was sent from God unto a city of Galilee, named Nazareth, to a virgin espoused to a man whose name was Joseph, of the house of David; and the virgin's name was Mary. And the angel came in unto her, and said, 'Hail, you that are highly favored, the Lord is with you: blessed are you among women.' And when she saw him, she was troubled at his saying, and considered in her mind what manner of greeting this should be. And the angel said unto her, 'Fear not, Mary: for you have found favor with God. And, behold, you shall conceive in your womb, and bring forth a*

son, and shall call his name JESUS. He shall be great, and shall be called the Son of the Highest: and the Lord God shall give unto him the throne of his father David: And he shall reign over the house of Jacob forever; and of his kingdom there shall be no end.'

Then said Mary unto the angel, 'How shall this be, seeing I know not a man?' And the angel answered and said unto her, 'The Holy Spirit shall come upon you, and the power of the Highest shall overshadow you: therefore also that holy thing which shall be born of you shall be called the Son of God. And, behold, your cousin Elizabeth, she has also conceived a son in her old age: and this is the sixth month with her, who was called barren. For with God nothing shall be impossible.' And Mary said,' Behold the handmaid of the Lord; be it unto me according to your word.' And the angel departed from her.

Luke 1:26-38

The angel Gabriel came to Mary, the mother of Jesus, and said, "Mary you're going to have a baby!" The King James says, "you shall *conceive*..."

Notice Mary's response was not one of unbelief but one with a knowledge of natural processes: "That's impossible," she said, "I'm a virgin!" The angel gave Mary a very practical explanation for this very supernatural event, "The power of the Highest shall overshadow you...the holy one to be born will be called the Son of God."

Mary received the Word spoken by the angel and said, "Be it unto me according to thy word." Mary believed the Word and *conceived* the Promise.

It is important that we believe the Word, but we must also *conceive* the Word. How does this process of conception take place? Scripture tells us to:

> *Pay attention to my words. Open your ears to what I say. Do not lose sight of these things. Keep them deep within your heart.*
>
> Proverbs 4:20-21 (God's Word)

> *For they are life unto those that find them, and health to all their flesh. Keep your heart with all diligence; for out of it are the issues of life.*
>
> Proverbs 4:22-23

> *Blessed is the man that walks not in the counsel of the ungodly, nor stands in the way of sinners, nor sits in the seat of the scornful. But his delight is in the law of the LORD; and in his law does he meditate day and night.*

> *And he shall be like a tree planted by the rivers of water, that brings forth its fruit in its season; his leaf also shall not wither; and whatsoever he does shall prosper.*
>
> Psalm 1:1-3

We must learn to guard our hearts and meditate on the Word. When we mediate on the Word, it's like watering a seed, it allows the Word to germinate and grow. If we don't guard what's going into our hearts, and retrain our minds to think like God thinks, we will get a harvest we don't like!

We've been born of the Word, just like James 1:18 says, but God also wants us to be blessed by the Word.[2] He wants the Word to produce a harvest like itself in our lives. According to Scripture, the seed of the Word is planted in our hearts.

The Hebrew word for heart is the "inner man" or spirit. It is our spirits that receive the Word, and which is made new when we are born again.[3] It is our spirits that believe, and our spirits that hold the very life of God.[4] But where do we see that life played out? Where does harvest from the seed of the Word take place? It takes place in our bodies.

Our bodies are where we see the results of God's covenant of healing, provision, peace, and protection. Herein lies the problem for most Christians: there is a little something between the spirit and body known as your soul. Your soul is your mind, will, and emotions. It is *this* part of you that chooses and that must be renewed day by day.

> *And you've become a new person. This new person is continually renewed in knowledge to be like its Creator.*
>
> Colossians 3:10 (God's Word)

The battlefield is the mind. It is here where we must retrain ourselves with the seed of the Word. 1 Corinthians says that whenever we sow—whether we sow the Word, finances, or kindness—we're not sowing what *is* but what *will be*.[5] Natural seeds work the same way. You plant seed because of the promise of harvest. You plant looking forward to what *will be,* not begrudging what is.

When seed is planted, it goes through stages: germination, gestation, and harvest. Gestation must take place between germination and harvest if you want to reap fruit. During the T-I-M-E of gestation, the plant prepares itself to make more seeds.

Gestation is perhaps the most important and delicate stage of a plant's life. If it does not receive enough water during this stage, the plant will not produce to its potential. If a bad storm or damaging winds come along, the shallow root system of the new plant may not be able to hold it securely in the ground. If an untimely frost occurs, the tender plant will die.

Though the seed that was planted is obviously working, it is during this stage of gestation that the process of harvest can be aborted. For example, if you plant 100-day corn, and try to harvest at 60 days, you're going to find a cornstalk, possibly an ear with no fruit in it, and a tassel. You can dig it up at this point, or try to pull the ear, but you're not going to have a harvest of fruit: you've aborted the process of seed. There must be germination *and* gestation before you can have harvest.

When we're discussing spiritual things, germination is the part of the cycle that takes place in our spirits. When we hear the Word and believe it, seed is planted by the Spirit of God into our spirits to begin the process of harvest. The seed begins to sprout, but before the intended harvest can take place, gestation is required.

The word "gestation" comes from the Latin word "to carry" and is defined as the "period of time before birth during which development occurs." It is the time of seed between germination and harvest.

Spiritually speaking, gestation occurs in our souls. Gestation is T-I-M-E. It is during this time when we must meditate on the Word that has been planted in our spirits, protecting and nurturing that seed. It is during this "carrying time" that the process can be aborted through circumstances, wrong teaching, and unbelief. We must protect our seed and water it with faith.

Remember that Hebrew word *hagah*? This is the time of meditation, the critical time during which we need to "think on these things."

> *Finally, brethren, whatsoever things are true, whatsoever things are honest, whatsoever things are just, whatsoever things are pure, whatsoever things are lovely, whatsoever things are of good report; if there be any virtue, and if there be any praise, think on these things.*
>
> Philippians 4:8

For in doing so we will discover the natural fruit or result of seed: the manifestation (or harvest) of what we are believing for.

> *...meditate [the Word] day and night, that you may observe to do according to all that is written therein: for then you shall make your way prosperous, and then you shall have good success.*
>
> Joshua 1:8

> *But his delight is in the law of the LORD; and in his law does he meditate day and night. And he shall be like a tree planted by the rivers of water, that brings forth its fruit in its season; his leaf also shall not wither; and whatsoever he does shall prosper.*
>
> Psalm 1:2-3

Many people may receive a Word from God, but most allow T-I-M-E to rob them of their harvest. Because they do not continue to protect and nourish that seed of the Word, the gestation process is aborted. When a Word is spoken to you, grab hold of that Word by faith, and continue to hold on to it, by faith, through the process of time.

If it didn't take faith—that unwavering knowledge that God's promise is yours regardless of what you see—then everyone would be born again, healed, and in heaven.

But the Lord said,

"Enter through the narrow gate. For wide is the gate and broad is the road that leads to destruction, and many enter through it. But small is the gate and narrow the road that leads to life, and only a few find it."

Matthew 7:13-14 (NIV)

God sows the seed of His Word in our spirits, but we know that it takes faith to enter into the things God's grace has provided. It takes faith to please Him.[6] God wants us to prosper. He wants us to have good success, but we have a part to play in it. Our part is during the time of gestation—our part is the meditation on His Word in our souls.

God says, "Here is My Word; this is My purpose—this is My plan. I want you to go and get it! Here's how: meditate the Word. Focus on the Word; do not let anything distract you. Speak the Word."

When we meditate on the Word, the process of gestation is taking place. The Word changes the thoughts and attitudes of our hearts, just like Hebrews says:

For the word of God is living and active. Sharper than any double-edged sword, it penetrates even to dividing soul and spirit, joints and marrow; it judges the thoughts and attitudes of the heart.

Hebrews 4:12 (NIV)

When we meditate on the Word, we are nourishing our seed. We are holding tight to it by faith, watering it, and protecting it. In this way, the seed of the Word will fulfill its time of gestation and move into the natural result—harvest. The seed of the Word will work in whatever area we allow it to complete its cycle. If we meditate the Word in the area of finances, we will see harvest come from that Word. If we meditate on the Word in the area of physical healing, we will see harvest in that area.

We must allow the Word of God to work in our minds through the conception period so we can see it work in our lives. This is the process of bringing forth fruit. We must believe and conceive the Word so we can inherit the Promise.[7]

---

[1] Romans 4:17
[2] Ephesians 1:3-6; Luke 11:28
[3] John 3:5; Luke 8:12,15; John 6:63
[4] Psalm119:11; Romans10:8; Romans 8:2,10, 11
[5] 1 Corinthians 15:37
[6] Hebrews 11:6; Romans 5:2
[7] Hebrews 6:12

CHAPTER EIGHT

A PICTURE LIKE THE WORD

What we see on the inside will always affect what we see on the outside. How we view God, and how we view ourselves, shapes the outcomes of our lives. We need to develop a picture like the Word.

In Genesis chapter 13, God spoke to Abraham. He said,

> *Lift up now your eyes, and look from the place where you are northward, and southward, and eastward, and westward: For all the land which you see, to you will I give it, and to your descendants forever… Arise, walk through the land in the length of it and in the breadth of it; for I will give it unto you.*
>
> Genesis 13:14-15, 17

God said, "Get up Abraham. Go look at the land and walk through it. Everything you *see* I will give to you." Abraham needed to see what God's grace had provided for him and his descendants before he could believe to possess it. Developing that visual picture—practicing the eye of faith—will help us to believe for and receive what God has promised to us as well. But if we can't see it, it is going to be difficult for us to possess it. The picture we see on the inside has the power to change the picture on the outside!

Three years before we moved to Colorado Springs, Barbara and I attended a conference in Denver where Mark Hankins was speaking about financial prosperity. Let me tell you, I heard some things that week that really challenged me. Mark was saying things that my natural mind, my upbringing, struggled with.

Now, I thought I believed in prosperity; I could see prosperity in the Word. I knew that it was God's will for me to prosper, to pay my bills, to take care of my family, but we were being challenged in a lot of those areas. While I believed the Word, and we did what we knew to do, I struggled to wrap my mind around how much God had for me and how little He worried about it. I couldn't get past the old concepts of "rubbing two nickels together," and "a penny saved is a penny earned." I had a picture in my mind, "Economize to Evangelize!"

Mark was saying some things that week that went way beyond where I was at the time. Barbara immediately grabbed hold of the Word, but all I could say was, "I don't know about that." It bothered me to think I wasn't operating at the level God had for me. I talked to Barbara about it, "I believe the Bible says God has prosperity in store for the righteous, but I think Mark is wrong in some areas. I think he may be a little overboard."

You have to understand, we didn't have *any* extra money. As a matter of fact, most months went farther than the money. We couldn't even afford to go to that meeting: a minister friend of ours had paid for our way. He paid for our hotel, our food—everything. I was doing all I knew to do, but the picture inside me was small.

Barbara, on the other hand, didn't have such a hard time changing her picture. She told me, "He's not wrong! I'm telling you, Mark is right. God wants to bless His children." God was beginning to work on my picture.

As we were leaving to go home that Saturday, we stopped at McDonald's. It was one of the cheapest places to eat back then. They had two quarter pounders for two dollars. I ordered for our family of five (Barbara, myself, and our three boys) because I didn't want anyone else spending my hard-earned money. I bought four quarter pounders for four dollars and one meal for three dollars. We got four waters and the drink from the meal.

After I ordered, I left to wash up. While I was gone, my wife prepared an illustrated sermon for me! Back at my table, there was sitting at my place a cup of water, a French fry box with one French fry, and my quarter pounder. I asked Barbara, "Where are my French fries?" She said, "You can be a one French fry man if you want to, but I believe that God has better. I believe that we can have more."

When we got home, I went back to our regular routine. Monday morning, I went for a run, as usual, and began mulling over everything Mark had said. Suddenly, the Lord spoke to me and said, "He's right. He's not wrong. You need to get a hold of that if I'm going to be able to do the work in your life that I have planned." What a wake-up call!

I began meditating on the Word in the area of finances. I was determined to allow God's Word to do its work. For six months I walked around quoting and personalizing these scriptures:

Praise you the LORD. Blessed is the man that fears the LORD, that delights greatly in his commandments. His descendants shall be mighty upon earth: the generation of the upright shall be blessed. Wealth and riches shall be in his house: and his righteousness endures forever. Unto the upright there arises light in the darkness: he is gracious, and full of compassion, and righteous. A good man shows favor, and lends: he will guide his affairs with discretion. Surely he shall not be moved forever: the righteous shall be in everlasting remembrance. He shall not be afraid of evil tidings: his heart is fixed, trusting in the LORD. His heart is established, he shall not be afraid, until he sees his desire upon his enemies.

Psalm 112:1-8

You that fear the LORD, trust in the LORD: he is their help and their shield. The LORD hath been mindful of us: he will bless us; he will bless the house of Israel; he will bless the house of Aaron. He will bless them that fear the LORD, both small and great. The LORD shall increase you more and more, you and your children. Ye are blessed of the LORD which made heaven and earth. The heaven, even the heavens, are the LORD's: but the earth hath he given to the children of men. The dead praise not the LORD, neither any that go down into silence. But we will bless the LORD from this time forth and for evermore. Praise the LORD.

Psalm 115:11-18

And it shall come to pass, if you shall hearken diligently unto the voice of the LORD your God, to observe and to do all his commandments which

I command you this day, that the LORD your God will set you on high above all nations of the earth: And all these blessings shall come on you, and overtake you, if you shall hearken unto the voice of the LORD your God.

Blessed shall you be in the city, and blessed shall you be in the field. Blessed shall be the fruit of your body, and the fruit of your ground, and the fruit of your herds, the increase of your cattle, and the flocks of your sheep. Blessed shall be your basket and your kneading-trough.

Blessed shall you be when you come in, and blessed shall you be when you go out. The LORD shall cause your enemies that rise up against you to be defeated before your face: they shall come out against you one way, and flee before you seven ways.

The LORD shall command the blessing upon you in your storehouses, and in all that you set your hand unto; and he shall bless you in the land which the LORD your God gives you. The LORD shall establish you a holy people unto himself, as he has sworn unto you, if you shall keep the commandments of the LORD your God, and walk in his ways.

And all people of the earth shall see that you are called by the name of the LORD; and they shall be afraid of you. And the LORD shall make you bountiful in goods, in the fruit of your body, and in the fruit of your cattle, and in the fruit of your ground, in the land which the LORD swore unto your fathers to give you. The LORD shall open unto you his good treasure, the heaven to give the rain unto your land in its season, and to bless all the work of your hand: and you shall lend unto many nations, and you shall not borrow.

And the LORD shall make you the head, and not the tail; and you shall be above only, and you shall not be beneath; if that you hearken unto the commandments of the LORD your God, which I command you this day, to observe and to do them: And you shall not go aside from any of the words which I command you this day, to the right hand, or to the left, to go after other gods to serve them.

Deuteronomy 28:1-14

I would say, "Praise the Lord. I am blessed because I delight in God's commands. My seed will be mighty on the earth. Wealth and riches will be in my house. My heart is fixed, trusting in the Lord. I will not be afraid."

It took me a period of time, but as I walked around my church speaking the Word, I overhauled the way that I thought about money. The Word of God changed the picture inside me about financial prosperity, and because the picture on the inside of me changed, the picture on the outside had no choice but to follow!

We're using an example here of prosperity, but this will work in any area of life, any area of God's Covenant. It will work for healing, for provision, for peace. It will work for favor and divine protection. The Word works when we believe it. The Word will come to pass in our lives, but how we see ourselves can limit the potential of its power. Proverbs 23 says, "as [a man] thinks in his heart, so is he."[1] We need to create a picture inside us that is like the Word. Jesus shared this principle with us in Matthew:

Jesus called the crowd to him and said, "Listen and understand. What goes into a man's mouth does not make him 'unclean,' but what comes out of his mouth, that is what makes him 'unclean.'"

Then the disciples came to him and asked, "Do you know that the Pharisees were offended when they heard this?" He replied, "Every plant that my heavenly Father has not planted will be pulled up by the roots. Leave them; they are blind guides. If a blind man leads a blind man, both will fall into a pit."

Peter said, "Explain the parable to us."

"Are you still so dull?" Jesus asked them. "Don't you see that whatever enters the mouth goes into the stomach and then out of the body? But the things that come out of the mouth come from the heart, and these make a man 'unclean.' For out of the heart come evil thoughts, murder, adultery, sexual immorality, theft, false testimony, slander. These are what make a man 'unclean'; but eating with unwashed hands does not make him 'unclean.'"

Matthew 15:10-20 (NIV)

It seems like people were constantly being offended by Jesus' words. Here, the Pharisees, the people who dotted every "i" and crossed every "t," the legalists of the day, were caught in their hypocrisy yet again. They thought they knew the Word, but Jesus said, "You have no relationship with the Word. You do not truly understand Its principles." They were focused on legalism, the ritual doing, rather than relationship with God.

Jesus' disciples said, "Master, the Pharisees are offended. You just spoke against everything they say is important." Jesus answered, "They don't belong to my Father. Leave them alone; they're blind leaders of the blind. They won't figure it out until they fall down." Jesus was saying religious rites and acts aren't going to do you any good; the Father is after your heart!

Jesus' entire ministry was about changing people's perception of the Father, of His Word. He was always saying things that would force people to evaluate their mindsets and look deeply into their hearts.[2] He wanted believers to change their thinking. Jesus knew that life and death was a result of the heart; those hidden attitudes and responses to God.[3]

To experience all that God has for us, we have to allow the Word to change the picture inside of us. We *are* blessed by the Lord, the Maker of heaven and Earth;[4] we need to see ourselves as blessed.

Psalm 115 says, "The heavens are the Lord's, but the Earth He has given to the children of men."[5] This is our place! The Earth is our place of authority, the place God has given to us.[6] We must begin to picture ourselves as God sees us and walk in the authority He has given us so that we can operate in faith.

We need to take authority in this realm so we can have what God said we can have, go where God tells us to go, do what God tells us to do, and be who God has called us to be. We cannot allow our upbringings, our traditions, our circumstances, or other people to hold us back from what the Lord has for us![7]

1 Proverbs 23:7
2 Matthew 5:19-6:21
3 Matthew 15:19; Mark7:21
4 Psalm 115:15
5 Psalm 115:16
6 Genesis 1:28
7 1 Corinthians 2:9-10, 16

PART THREE

THE PURPOSE OF THE WORD

For the word of God is alive and powerful. It is sharper than the sharpest two-edged sword, cutting between soul and spirit, between joints and marrow. It exposes our innermost thoughts and desires.

Hebrews 4:12 (NLT)

CHAPTER NINE
THE WORD IS FOOD

The purpose of the Word goes beyond our receiving it; it goes beyond our rebirth and the revelation of our new character. According to the psalmist, the Word of God is "light to our eyes."[1] Have you ever tried to maneuver through your living room in the middle of the night without turning on the lights? While you may have a general idea of where you're going, you go slowly, trying not to stub a toe or bruise a knee. Turning on a light, however, allows you to move freely about the room, avoiding obstacles and that spare Lego that fell under the end table.

God's Word works in the same way. The light of the Word eliminates life's uncertainties; it gives us confidence (like a light bulb in a dark room) in the direction we should go.

The Word of God is also food for our spirits and a mirror for our souls. It shows us the difference between what's coming from of our heads and what's coming from our spirits. Once we have allowed the Word of God to change our minds and believed that what It says about us is true, we must continue to feed ourselves with the Word. We cannot be deceived into thinking that we have completed "our part" and that the rest is up to God.

Jesus compared the importance of the Word of God to food on several occasions. He said the Word was as important to our spirits as bread (or food) is to our bodies. When Satan came to tempt Jesus in the wilderness, he targeted his attack on Jesus' identity. He said, "If you be the Son of God…"

Satan tempts us the same way: by getting us to question who we are (that new creation in Christ)[2] or what God has said.[3] He tries to distract us from God's purpose by moving our focus onto our circumstances.

Notice that Jesus countered Satan's attack with the Word. He quoted, "Man shall not live by bread alone, but by every word that proceeds out of the mouth of God."[4] He was essentially saying, "My circumstances (whether or not I'm hungry) will not move me. Only the voice of God will change my direction."[5] Jesus had heard the Word that He was the Son of God, but He continued to feed Himself with that Word (or focus on it), so that when He was tempted, He remained strong. Just like bread strengthens our bodies, the Word of God is our spirits' source of life and strength:

> But those who trust in the LORD will find new strength. They will soar high on wings like eagles. They will run and not grow weary. They will walk and not faint.
>
> Isaiah 40:31 (NLT)

> Take to your heart all the words with which I am warning you today, which you shall command your sons to observe carefully, even all the words of this law. For it is not an idle word for

*you; indeed it is your life. And by this word you
will prolong your days in the land, which you are
about to cross the Jordan to possess.*

Deuteronomy 32:46-47 (NASB)

*Turn my eyes from worthless things, and give me
life through your word...Your promise preserves
my life.*

Psalm 119:37, 50 (NIV)

At another time in Jesus' ministry, recorded in John
chapter four, the disciples came to Him to urge Him to eat.
They had been traveling all day and were tired. But when
they stopped to rest, Jesus began to minister to the woman
at the well. At her testimony, people gathered to see Jesus,
and His disciples became worried:

*So the people came streaming from the village
to see him. Meanwhile, the disciples were urging
Jesus, "Rabbi, eat something." But Jesus replied, "I have a kind of food you know nothing
about." "Did someone bring him food while we
were gone?" the disciples asked each other.*

John 4:30-33 (NLT)

Jesus' concern was for the spiritual well-being of the
people; His actions loudly spoke, "this Word of Truth is more
important than food for my tired body." The Word of God is
the most important influence in our Christian walk. It is our
spiritual food. Psalm 34 says to "taste and see that the Lord
is good."[6] How can we experience or recognize the
goodness of God but through His Word?

It is the Word of God that shows us who God is[7] and what
He says He will do.[8] It is the Word that teaches us who we
are[9] and the good plan that God has in store for our lives.[10]
Peter declares that after receiving the grace of God, it is

through His Word that we "grow up" and mature in our salvation.

> *As newborn babes, desire the sincere milk of the word, that ye may grow thereby: If so be ye have tasted that the Lord is gracious.*
>
> 1 Peter 2:2-3

Without the Word of God to teach and train us in the way of righteousness we will not mature in our understanding of who Christ is in us.

Perhaps you've seen a group of Christians walking around with their spiritual Pampers on. They are zealous, but don't understand spirit, soul, and body. They try to stand and fight against the enemy without an understanding of their authority in Christ.

It is easy for these babies to fall into condemnation and/or legalism. It is easy for them to allow the "cares of this world and the deceitfulness of wealth" to choke out the seed that has been planted in them.[11] That is why Jesus said to "make disciples."[12]

A disciple is a "disciplined student," not a mere follower, but one who studies and obeys the teachings of another, often teaching others to do likewise. To be a true disciple, we must continue in the Word.[13] Without it, we cannot grow like the author of Hebrews says:

> *You have been believers so long now that you ought to be teaching others. Instead, you need someone to teach you again the basic things about God's word. You are like babies who need milk and cannot eat solid food.*
>
> Hebrews 5:12 (NLT)

The Word of God is essential to our spiritual maturity!

Paul said:

I have fed you with milk, and not with solid food: for until now you were not able to bear it, neither yet now are you able… For you are yet carnal…
1 Corinthians 3:2, 3

Paul says that when we are carnal (thinking and acting with only the natural mind and uncontrolled emotions—those same things that drive the decisions of the world) we are spiritually immature, mere "infants in Christ."

For those who live according to the flesh set their minds on the things of the flesh, but those who live according to the Spirit set their minds on the things of the Spirit. To focus our minds on the human nature leads to death, but to focus our minds on the Spirit leads to life and peace. That is why the mind that focuses on human nature is hostile toward God. It refuses to submit to the authority of God's law because it is powerless to do so.
Romans 8:5-7 (ISV)

We must feed ourselves with the Word of God so that we can know who He has made us to be and the freedom of that life's calling.[14] We must remember the importance of the Word as our spiritual food and allow the Word to nurture us into maturity. Ephesians says:

*It was he who gave some to be apostles, some to be prophets, some to be evangelists, and some to be pastors and teachers, to prepare God's people for works of service, so that the body of Christ may be built up until we all reach unity in the faith and in the knowledge of the Son of God and become **mature**, attaining to the*

> *whole measure of the fullness of Christ. Then we will no longer be infants, tossed back and forth by the waves, and blown here and there by every wind of teaching and by the cunning and craftiness of men in their deceitful scheming. Instead, speaking the truth in love, we will in all things grow up into him who is the Head, that is, Christ.*
>
> Ephesians 4:11-15 (NIV, emphasis mine)

When we become mature, Paul says, "attaining to the whole measure of the fullness of Christ," we will find ourselves steadfast and confident in the goodness of God, not easily moved by winds of change and challenge. Like the psalmist, our belief will hold us steadfast in the face of adversity.[15] Our maturity in the Word will enable us to easily distinguish good from evil, carnality from spirituality.

> *Solid food is for the mature, who by constant use have trained themselves to distinguish good from evil.*
>
> Hebrews 5:14 (NIV)

Notice that it is by "constant use" that this maturity happens. We cannot expect to grow without a regular, intentional exposure to the Word. If our bodies need food on a regular basis, wouldn't our spirits? Let us acknowledge our dependence on the Word of God. Let us grow in grace and the knowledge of Christ.[16]

And:

> *Leaving elementary instruction about the Christ, let us advance to mature manhood and not be continually re-laying a foundation of repentance from lifeless works and of faith in God, or of teaching about ceremonial washings, the laying*

on of hands, the resurrection of the dead, and the last judgment.

Hebrews 4:1-2 (Weymouth)

We must realize the power and life in the Word of God. We must see that Its purpose is for our benefit. We must let the Word of God become our source of strength so that we may take territory for the Kingdom of God!

---

[1] Psalm 19:8; 119:105

[2] 2 Corinthians 5:17

[3] Genesis 3:1

[4] Matthew 4:4; Deuteronomy 8:3

[5] Matthew 4:1-11

[6] Psalm 34:8

[7] Genesis 22:14; Exodus 15:26; Joshua 6:24; Exodus 17:15; Exodus 31:13; Jeremiah 23:6; Ezekiel 48:35

[8] Isaiah 59:16, 20-21; Psalm 89:34

[9] Romans 8:15; Galatians 3:26-4:7; 2 Corinthians 5:15-20

[10] Jeremiah 29:11; 1 Corinthians 2:12; 2 Corinthians 2:9-10

[11] Mark 4:19

[12] Matthew 28:19

[13] Proverbs 7:2; John 8:31, 14:21

[14] Galatians 3:23-29

[15] Psalm 27:13

[16] 2 Peter 3:18

CHAPTER TEN

THE WORD IS OUR DEFENSE

According to Hebrews chapter four, the Word of God is "alive and powerful and sharper than any two-edged sword." The Word is a powerful weapon to use against the enemy; it helps us walk in the victory that Christ has provided. There is power and life in the Word!

Let's take a look at the last recorded picture of Jesus, the Word made flesh,[1] in the Scripture, and notice how He used this "two-edged sword."

The book of Revelation was written by the apostle John while he was in exile on the island of Patmos. During this time, the Roman government began to persecute the Church with relish: executing preachers and apostles, making worship of the emperor mandatory, and rounding up Christians to feed them to the lions during Roman games.

The apostle John, the last eyewitness of Jesus, was sentenced to death by the Roman emperor for leading a rebellion. They intended to kill him by throwing him into boiling oil/tar, but John came out unscathed. Still trying to get rid of him, John was sent to Patmos where there wasn't anyone for him to lead.[2] (Patmos, a tiny lump of rock off the coast of modern Turkey, was used by the Romans as a penal settlement.) Here, Revelation chapter one tells us that John continued to live as he always had—by the Truth—and God rewarded and encouraged him with this revelation of Christ and the time to come:

> *I John, who also am your brother, and companion in tribulation, and in the kingdom and patience of Jesus Christ, was in the isle that is called Patmos, for the word of God, and for the testimony of Jesus Christ. I was in the Spirit on the Lord's day, and heard behind me a great voice, as of a trumpet, Saying, 'I am Alpha and Omega, the first and the last: and, What you see, write in a book, and send it unto the seven churches which are in Asia; unto Ephesus, and unto Smyrna, and unto Pergamum, and unto Thyatira, and unto Sardis, and unto Philadelphia, and unto Laodicea.'*

> *And I turned to see the voice that spoke with me. And being turned, I saw seven golden lampstands; And in the midst of the seven lampstands one like unto the Son of man, clothed with a garment down to the foot, and girded about the breast with a golden belt. His head and his hair were white like wool, as white as snow; and his eyes were as a flame of fire; And his feet like unto fine bronze, as if they burned in a furnace; and his voice as the sound of many waters.*

> *And he had in his right hand seven stars: and out of his mouth went a sharp two edged sword: and his countenance was as the sun shines in its*

strength. And when I saw him, I fell at his feet as dead. And he laid his right hand upon me, saying unto me, 'Fear not; I am the first and the last: I am He that lives, and was dead; and, behold, I am alive forevermore, Amen; and have the keys of hades and of death. Write the things which you have seen, and the things which are, and the things which shall be hereafter...'

Revelation 1:9-19

When Christ appeared to John in His glorified state, John said, "out of His mouth [went] a sharp double-edged sword." In Revelation 19, John records Christ returning to Earth to rule and reign, judging and making war.[3]

Jesus is coming back, but He will not come meekly, as a little baby—this time He will come as King! John says of that day, "every eye will see Him, even those who pierced Him."[4] Jesus is coming back to set things straight on the Earth. Chapter 19 describes Jesus in His glorified state and says, "out of His mouth goes a sharp sword..." This sword is the Word of God.[5] The Lord spoke to me once when I was studying about this and said, "One edge of the Word is for defense, the other for offense!"

Right now, let's focus on how the Word defends us. God gave us His Word to use, and He gave us Jesus as our example. Let's look in Matthew, immediately after Jesus was baptized. He was about 30 years old at this time, ready to begin His public ministry. Here we see that Jesus had identified with God's calling for His life, and scripture says He was "led by the Spirit into the wilderness to be tempted by the devil."

And when He had fasted forty days and forty nights, He was afterward hungry. And when the tempter came to Him, he said, 'If you are the Son of God, command that these stones be made bread.' But He answered and said, 'It is written, Man shall not live by bread alone, but by every word that proceeds out of the mouth of God.'

Then the devil took Him up into the holy city, and set Him on a pinnacle of the temple, And said unto Him, 'If you are the Son of God, cast yourself down: for it is written, He shall give his angels charge concerning you: and in their hands they shall bear you up, lest at any time you dash your foot against a stone.' Jesus said unto him, 'It is written again, You shall not test the Lord your God.'

Again, the devil took Him up into an exceedingly high mountain, and showed Him all the king-doms of the world, and the glory of them; And said unto Him, 'All these things will I give you, if you will fall down and worship me.' Then said Je-sus unto him, 'Be gone, Satan: for it is written, You shall worship the Lord your God, and him only shall you serve.' Then the devil left Him, and, behold, angels came and ministered unto Him.

Matthew 4:2-11

Notice how Satan chose to appear at Jesus' hour of weakness: the Scripture says, "He was hungry." Notice, too, how Satan always began his barrage of attack with "*if* you are the Son of God." Although only one month before, God had audibly spoken from heaven, "You are my beloved Son...,"[6] Satan began each of his assaults by attacking Jesus' identity. He nearly always tries tempting us in this way too. Why? Because if he can get us to question who we are, who God is, or what we have from God, he can wreak havoc in our lives. He is always on the attack, ready to try to steal from us what God has spoken. Just like in the Parable of the Sower, he is looking for any seed he can gobble up to keep from spouting and producing a harvest.[7]

Now remember, at this time, Jesus was hungry. How many of us miss a meal or start a fast and soon notice that our flesh begins to talk to us? Jesus had gone 40 days without food! Now don't think that because He was Christ He was without the struggles common to us. Hebrews tells us that Jesus was a man—just as we are. He knew our every weakness and temptation because He experienced them all Himself.[8] I don't know where people get the idea that life was easier for Jesus because He had a different nature than ours, but it is wrong!

Jesus was born without the seed of sin—like the first Adam—but He was still a man. He still had to learn obedience and choose to do right[9] (and we all know how well Adam did with that!). So, I know that after 40 days of fasting, Jesus' flesh was speaking to Him. But He didn't let that sway Him. He answered each of Satan's attacks from His spirit, with the Truth of the Word, and said, "It is written..."

The enemy may come against us and try to tempt us, but hit him back with the Word! Defend yourself with the scripture. Don't just hit him once, beat him with it, and keep hitting him until he leaves you alone! He may regroup to try again, but we have a great weapon! Remember, if the devil can get our focus off our identity in Christ, then it will be easy for him to lead us into temptation.

Satan came to Jesus and said, "If you are the Son of God...," but Jesus always countered with the Word. The second time Satan brought the attack, he tried to use the Word of God to deceive Jesus saying, "Throw yourself down. *For it is written*: 'He will command his angels concerning you, and they will lift you up in their hands, so that you will not strike your foot against a stone.'"

You know, Satan doesn't have any new tricks; he just puts them in a different bag and brings them again. What did he do in the Garden? He twisted the Word of God.[10] He'll try to do the same thing again. When you start speaking the Word, he may try to take that Word and twist it up. But you speak right back, just like Jesus did, "It is written again, you shall not tempt the Lord your God." Jesus just kept relying on the Word of God as His defense. He said, "I know what the Word says, you can't deceive me."

The third time Satan struck, he struck hard. On top of a high mountain, Satan showed Jesus all the kingdoms of the world and their glory. He said, "All this I will give you if you will bow down and worship me." Now, Satan is the god of this world, he had the splendor of the world's systems to give. In this attack, he was essentially saying, "We can bypass God's plan and make our own, Jesus. You can have all this back without the pain of the cross."

But Jesus did not even entertain the idea. He said, "Away from me, Satan!" Don't carry on a conversation with the devil; don't allow the seeds he plants to take root. Take your authority and abort that process! Don't allow your mind to wallow in 'should haves' and 'what ifs.' Don't stay in pride or self-pity. RUN! Get out of there, whatever it takes!

Sometimes people put themselves into positions that they don't need to get involved in. If you find yourself in that situation, do what Joseph did: take that window of escape[11] and run![12] Use your brain; don't be stupid.

I'm full of the Holy Spirit, I'm a preacher of the Gospel, but I have a body, and I know that body is capable of stupidity. Sometimes I have to turn my head, sometimes I have to run. Know the Word and use wisdom. There are some things you just don't need to be involved in and some places you don't need to go. Take your authority and tell the devil to "shut up and get out in the name of Jesus!"

Use the Word like the weapon of defense it is. Take control of your thoughts and begin to see things from God's perspective. How do you defeat the devil? How do you fight a spiritual enemy? With a spiritual weapon: the Word of God.

> *For the weapons of our warfare are not carnal, but mighty through God to the pulling down of strongholds.*
>
> 2 Corinthians 10:4

Remember the Word is our defense:

> *You are my refuge and my shield; your word is my source of hope.*
>
> Psalm 119:114 (NLT)

> *God's way is perfect. All the LORD's promises prove true. He is a shield for all who look to him for protection.*
>
> Psalm 18:30 (NLT)

> *Happy are you, O Israel! Who is like you, a people saved by the LORD, the shield of your help, and the sword of your triumph!*
>
> Deuteronomy 33:29 (ESV)

> *We faithfully preach the truth. God's power is working in us. We use the weapons of righteous-*

> *ness in the right hand for attack and the left hand*
> *for defense.*
>
> 2 Corinthians 6:7 (NLT)

Jesus gave us authority over the devil, there is no need to fear.[13] Dr. Lester Sumrall was once in a foreign nation ministering when he woke up in the night and noticed the devil had moved his bed across the room while he was sleeping. He didn't get nervous. He didn't ignore it. He just said, "Devil, put it back!" And "Bam!" the bed slid back across the room and hit the wall. Don't let the devil mess around in your territory; don't let him intimidate you!

Once when Smith Wigglesworth was in a foreign nation, he woke up and saw the devil at the end of his bed. "Oh, it's only you," he said and went back to sleep!

I heard another story about a missionary in Africa who went to a village where they had never heard the Gospel. There was a witch doctor there who the whole village respected. He came to the missionary and said, "Let's have a contest to see whose God is bigger." The missionary agreed and they settled on a day and time. After announcing it to the village, the witch doctor left to prepare. He fasted and prayed and worked himself into a tizzy, but the missionary just went about his normal business.

At the appointed time, the entire village assembled to watch. The witch doctor lay down on the ground and began chanting; soon he was levitating. The missionary asked God, "What do I do?" God said, "Go put your foot on him and tell him to come down in the Name of Jesus." So, the man did. Boom! That witch doctor fell to the ground, not even knowing where he was or what was happening, but the whole village saw the power of God and came to Jesus!

We are here to demonstrate the lordship of Jesus Christ! Jesus is Lord in heaven; He is Lord on Earth. Jesus is Lord in hell—He conquered the devil and won the victory![14] We are here to make Jesus' lordship known in the Earth. How do we do it? By the power and life of God's Word.

Begin to say, with your mouth, the things that agree with the Word of God. Know who you are and take your authority! Use the Word of God in defense when the enemy comes to attack. Jesus has already won the victory!

So shall they fear the name of the LORD from the west, and his glory from the rising of the sun. When the enemy shall come in like a flood, the Spirit of the LORD shall lift up a standard against him.

Isaiah 59:19

---

[1] John 1:14

[2] Foxe, J. 2012. *Foxes Book of Martyrs.* Trinity Press.

[3] Revelation 19:11-14

[4] Revelation 1:7

[5] Ephesians 6:17

[6] Matthew 3:17

[7] Matthew 13:1-23

[8] Hebrews 2:17-18; Hebrews 4:15; Hebrews 5:2

[9] Isaiah 7:14-15; Luke 2:52

[10] Genesis 3:1

[11] 2 Corinthians 10:13

[12] Genesis 39:12

[13] Ephesians 4:8; Colossians 2:15

[14] Ephesians 4:8

CHAPTER ELEVEN

THE WORD IS OUR OFFENSE

Defense is essential to our survival as a Christian, but it's difficult to win without offense. For example, how do you win a football game if all you do is play defense? How can you win if nobody scores any points, if the offense is never used? I suppose it might be possible, but your team is going to come off the field hot and sweaty, tired and bruised, some may be so broken and downcast they're ready to quit. It's a lot more fun to play when you can see yourself winning!

In sports, the best way to win is to have a team with both good defense and good offense; someone who protects the ball and someone who knows how to use the ball. It's much easier for a team's defense to stay focused on the field if they can see that their sacrifice is worth something, if they can see that their team is winning. Good sports teams know the importance of both a good defense *and* a good offense. Unfortunately, a lot of Christians do not.

Paul, in Ephesians chapter six, gives us great insight into all that Christ has provided for our defense against Satan and the war he is waging for our souls.

> *Therefore put on the full armor of God, so that when the day of evil comes, you may be able to stand your ground, and after you have done everything, to stand. Stand firm then, with the belt of truth buckled around your waist, with the breastplate of righteousness in place, and with your feet fitted with the readiness that comes from the gospel of peace. In addition to all this, take up the shield of faith, with which you can extinguish all the flaming arrows of the evil one. Take the helmet of salvation and the sword of the Spirit, which is the word of God. And pray in the Spirit on all occasions with all kinds of prayers and requests. With this in mind, be alert and always keep on praying for all the saints.*
>
> Ephesians 6:13-18 (NIV)

Notice verse 17 lists one vital piece of that armor from God that many Christians forget about—"the sword of the Spirit, which is the Word of God." A lot of Christians walk around only playing defense—trying to dodge Satan's darts, allowing their shield and breastplate to deflect all his attacks. They stand still against the onslaught of the enemy hoping they can keep standing until the bell sounds.

But we don't want to just "make it" to the end. We don't want to leave the field early because we're beat up and tired; we don't even want to walk away limping. We want to experience all that God has for us,[1] to experience His victory! Using our tools of defense against the enemy (resisting the devil,[2] knowing who you are in Christ,[3] using your faith,[4] etc.) are good, but let's not forget that God has provided everything we need to live that overcoming life. He has provided for our offense as well as our defense!

His divine power has given us everything we need for life and godliness through our knowledge of him who called us by his own glory and goodness… For this very reason, make every effort to add to your faith goodness; and to goodness, knowledge; and to knowledge, self-control; and to self-control, perseverance; and to perseverance, godliness; and to godliness, brotherly kindness; and to brotherly kindness, love.

For if you possess these qualities in increasing measure, they will keep you from being ineffective and unproductive in your knowledge of our Lord Jesus Christ. But if anyone does not have them, he is nearsighted and blind, and has forgotten that he has been cleansed from his past sins. Therefore, my brothers, be all the more eager to make your calling and election sure. For if you do these things, you will never fall, and you will receive a rich welcome into the eternal kingdom of our Lord and Savior Jesus Christ.

2 Peter 1:3, 5-11 (NIV)

I give you this instruction in keeping with the prophecies once made about you, so that by following them you may fight the good fight holding on to faith and a good conscience. Some have rejected these and so have shipwrecked their faith.

Timothy 1:18-19 (NIV)

But the Lord is faithful; he will strengthen you [for offense] *and guard you* [in defense] *from the evil one.*

2 Thessalonians 3:3 (NLT, brackets mine)

A key to experiencing victory in the Christian life is by taking advantage of all that God has provided for us. He did not leave us unequipped!

> *Now the God of peace, who brought up from the dead the great Shepherd of the sheep through the blood of the eternal covenant, even Jesus our Lord, equip you in every good thing to do His will, working in us that which is pleasing in His sight, through Jesus Christ, to whom be the glory forever and ever. Amen.*
>
> Hebrews 13:20-21 (NASB)

> *All Scripture is God-breathed and is useful for teaching, rebuking, correcting and training in righteousness, so that the man of God may be thoroughly equipped for every good work.*
>
> Timothy 3:16-17 (NIV)

> *For it is God who is producing in you both the desire and the ability to do what pleases him.*
>
> Philippians 2:13 (ISV)

What did Paul say was used to "equip us for every good work"? The Word! There is only one offensive weapon listed in Ephesians six, and that is the Word of God. We must learn to rely on the power and life in the Word and use it from an offensive position.

In a good sporting match, the offense doesn't start playing only after the defense is beaten up and tired. They work together! Spiritually, we don't have to wait until everything is falling apart before we begin to believe God and stand on His Word. We can believe God all the time. We don't have to wait until our children are making all the wrong choices before we start to believe God for our children. We start teaching them the principals of God's Word while they're young, praying for them and believing God for them before they start stretching their wings of independence.

I used to put my children to bed when they were little and cover them up, laying my hands on them and saying, "Father, I thank You for keeping my children in good health, for keeping them strong. I know your angels are watching over them, keeping them in all their ways. Thank You that they are blessed, and that You are making them a good witness for Jesus." Barbara and I would stand on scriptures of health and safety for our family.

Scriptures like:

> *And you shall serve the LORD your God, and he shall bless your bread, and your water; and I will take sickness away from the midst of you.*
>
> Exodus 23:25

> *If you make the Most High your dwelling—even the LORD, who is my refuge—then no harm will befall you, no disaster will come near your tent. For he will command his angels concerning you to guard you in all your ways; they will lift you up in their hands, so that you will not strike your foot against a stone. You will tread upon the lion and the cobra; you will trample the great lion and the serpent. "Because he loves me," says the LORD, "I will rescue him; I will protect him, for he acknowledges my name.*
>
> Psalm 91:9-14 (NIV)

We stood on scriptures of prosperity and favor too:

> *The just man walks in his integrity: his children are blessed after him.*
>
> Proverbs 20:7

> *May the favor of the Lord our God rest upon us;*
> *establish the work of our hands for us--yes,*
> *establish the work of our hands.*
>
> Psalm 19:17 (NIV)

> *His seed shall be mighty upon earth: the*
> *generation of the upright shall be blessed.*
>
> Psalm 112:2

> *I have been young, and now am old; yet have I*
> *not seen the righteous forsaken, nor his offspring*
> *begging bread. He is ever merciful, and lends;*
> *and his descendants are blessed.*
>
> Psalm 37:25-26

The words that we spoke over our children and the scriptures we believed for them years ago are coming to pass in their lives. Our children are blessed by the Lord! They receive favor and walk in wisdom. They are experiencing His hand of blessing and honoring Him for it. Praise God!

We can use the Word of God offensively like this in every area of our lives. Let's be proactive. Before we are sick or struggling with lack, let's speak the Word over our lives and eliminate, shorten, or weaken Satan's attacks in those circumstances. For example, before sickness ever comes our way, we can believe and say, "No plague is coming near my dwelling.[5] I am the healed of the Lord.[6] Thank God I have health.[7] I have strength.[8] I'm doing the will of God."

Barbara and I run six mornings a week. When I run, I speak the Word. I say, "Thank you, Lord, I'm healthy. Thank You, I'm strong. My body is the temple of the Holy Ghost that You have given me. No sickness or disease can stay in my body…" Sometimes my body tells me different things, but I will not let my body rule me! I'm going to let my spirit rule me.

In the area of finances, we've been taught that if we're attacked and experiencing some challenges then we start speaking things like, "I have a covenant with God.[9] I'm blessed of the Lord, the maker of heaven and earth.[10] My God supplies all my needs according to His riches in glory by Christ Jesus."[11]

These things are right and good, but we can speak words that agree with what God says about us *all the time*, not just when we're experiencing challenges. We don't have to wait to believe God. We don't have to wait for the financial dilemma, or job loss. We can constantly be speaking the Word and experiencing the blessings of it!

This does not mean we will never face challenges, but by using the Word offensively, we will be better able to handle them when they do come.

> *No temptation has seized you except what is common to man. And God is faithful; he will not let you be tempted beyond what you can bear. But when you are tempted, he will also provide a way out so that you can stand up under it.*
>
> 1 Corinthians 10:13 (NIV)

> *If this is so, then the Lord knows how to rescue godly men from trials and to hold the unrighteous for the day of judgment...*
>
> 2 Peter 2:9 (NIV)

> *Let us hold tightly without wavering to the hope we affirm, for God can be trusted to keep his promise.*
>
> Hebrews 10:23 (NLT)

When faced with the possibility of walking alone, of going against the popular cries of his day, Joshua said it this way:

> *If serving the LORD seems undesirable to you, then choose for yourselves this day whom you will serve, whether the gods your forefathers served beyond the River, or the gods of the Amorites, in whose land you are living. But as for me and my household, we will serve the LORD.*
>
> Joshua 24:15 (NIV)

He essentially said, "I've already made up my mind. Before the temptation to trust my own strength comes, I've decided what I will do. I'm predestined to do what's right, to succeed, because I have made up my mind—before I go into the heat of battle—no matter what the rest of you choose, my family is going to serve the Lord." You see, if we make up our minds before we get into certain situations, there will be some places we won't go, some things we won't do.

Psalm 119 says,

> *How can a young man keep his way pure? By living according to your word. I seek you with all my heart; do not let me stray from your commands. I have hidden your word in my heart that I might not sin against you. Praise be to you, O LORD; teach me your decrees. With my lips I recount all the laws that come from your mouth. I rejoice in following your statutes as one rejoices in great riches. I meditate on your precepts and consider your ways. I delight in your decrees; I will not neglect your word.*
>
> Psalm 119:9-16 (NIV)

The psalmist is saying we can use the Word proactively to set boundaries. We hide it in our hearts beforehand (offensively) so what when the temptation comes, we already know how we'll respond. We've got to put the Word of God deep on the inside. If we hide the Word in our hearts, that Word will begin to change our thoughts, and eventually it will come out to produce life like itself.

The Bible says in Psalm 149, "Let the high praises of God be in their mouth and a two-edged sword in their hand."[12] The Hebrew word here is *pipiyoth,* which literally means "a two-mouthed" sword.[13] Hebrews repeats this phrase in chapter four:

> *For the word of God is alive and powerful. It is sharper than the sharpest two-edged sword, cutting between soul and spirit, between joint and marrow. It exposes our innermost thoughts and desires.*
>
> Hebrews 4:12 (NLT)

The Greek word here for "two-edged" sword, *distomon,* repeats the Hebrew phrase saying literally "two-mouthed."[14] What is this two-mouthed sword? It is the Word of God,[15] and according to these scriptures, this sword is designed to be used "in the mouth!" We need to speak the Word; it is a spiritual weapon!

One side of the Word of God is used for defense and the other is for offense.

We need to know the Word. It is more than just a book about God, it is more than simply His story: there is power and life in the Word! Jesus said,

> *The Spirit alone gives eternal life. Human effort accomplishes nothing. And the very words I have spoken to you are spirit and life.*
>
> John 6:63 (NLT)

Praise the Lord! The Word of God is our strength! It is eternal. We can count on God's Word. Jesus said, "Heaven and earth will pass away, but my words will never pass away."[16] God said,

> *So is my word that goes out from my mouth: It will not return to me empty, but will accomplish what I desire and achieve the purpose for which I sent it.*

> Isaiah 55:11

God has made every promise available to us with the intent to fulfill! We can take the Word of God to the bank! Years ago, banks did not insure the money people deposited with them. You could deposit with them, but if the bank was robbed or made bad investments with your money, it was you who was robbed, you who made the bad investment.

As a matter of fact, during the Great Depression, many banks began to fail because of bad investments. People worried that they would lose all their hard-earned cash, so thousands of depositors ran to their local banks to withdraw all their available funds. But banks didn't keep enough cash on hand for the demanded withdrawals, and panic ensued.

In order to restore the American people to faith in the economic system, President Roosevelt created the Federal Deposit Insurance Corporation. This new government body was to regulate the banking industry and ensure that every depositor (in participating banks) be guaranteed the return of their deposits even if their bank collapsed. Still today the FDIC promises "deposits backed by the full faith and credit of the United States Government."

As important as many Americans think that is, we, as believers, have a much better promise! The Lord God, Creator of the Universe, has backed His Word by the full force and honor of His Name![17]

Numbers says,

> *God is not a man, that he should lie, nor a son of man, that he should change his mind. Does he speak and then not act? Does he promise and not fulfill?*

Numbers 23:19

God honors His Word! But that Word can sit on a shelf, not accomplishing anything, if we don't rise up and take responsibility for our part. We must believe the Word to receive what it says is ours. We must see the Word as absolute truth and receive it with an attitude of meekness. We must allow the Word of God to teach us and change our perspective. We must begin to see what God sees and say what He says.

The Bible says, "whosoever is born of God, overcomes the world, and this is the victory that overcomes the world, even our faith."[18] If you have been born again, you have been made to win; you are a "whosoever!" You are an overcomer by the nature of God that is in you.

Start believing God, start using His Word, and act like who you are! Take your authority and refuse to accept what the world is saying: you speak what God says. Keep going forward in the name of Jesus and walk in the victory that God's grace has provided!

---

[1] Ephesians 1:17-19
[2] James 4:7
[3] 2 Peter 1:3; 2 Corinthians 5:17
[4] Hebrews 6:12; Romans 4:16; Romans 1:17
[5] Psalm 91
[6] Jeremiah 33:6
[7] Proverbs 4:22
[8] Isaiah 40:31
[9] Deuteronomy 8:18
[10] Psalm 115:15
[11] Philippians 4:19
[12] Psalm 149:6
[13] Strong's Hebrew Concordance: 6374 "PIPIYOTH"
[14] Greek Lexicon: Hebrews 4:12 line-by-line translation
[15] Ephesians 6:17
[16] Mark 13:31
[17] Psalm 138:2
[18] 1 John 5:4